CLIFFORD ODETS

An Annotated Bibliography

1935-1989

MECKLER'S LITERARY BIBLIOGRAPHIES

Walker Percy: A Bibliography: 1930-1984
by Stuart Wright
ISBN 0-88736-046-7 CIP 1986

The Bibliography of Contemporary American
Poetry, 1945-1985: An Annotated Checklist
by William McPheron
ISBN 0-88736-054-8 CIP 1986

Harry Crews: A Bibliography
by Michael Hargraves
ISBN 0-88736-060-2 CIP 1986

William Goyen: A Descriptive Bibliography,
1938-1985
by Stuart Wright
ISBN 0-88736-057-2 CIP 1986

Stevie Smith: A Bibliography
by Jack Barbera, William McBrien
& Helen Bajan
ISBN 0-88736-101-3 CIP 1987

Sylvia Plath: An Analytical Bibliography
by Stephen Tabor
ISBN 0-88736-100-5 CIP 1987

H. Rider Haggard: A Bibliography
by D.E. Whatmore
ISBN 0-88736-102-1 CIP 1987

Robert Gover: A Descriptive Bibliography
by Michael Hargraves
ISBN 0-88736-165-X CIP 1988

Confederate Broadside Poems:
An Annotated Descriptive Bibliography
by William Moss
ISBN 0-88736-163-3 CIP 1988

Alice Malsenior Walker:
An Annotated Bibliography: 1968-1986
by Louis H. Pratt and Darnell D. Pratt
ISBN 0-88736-156-0 CIP 1988

Supplement to A Bibliography of
George Moore
by Edwin Gilcher
ISBN 0-88736-199-4 CIP 1988

Alan Sillitoe: A Bibliography
by David Gerard
ISBN 0-88736-104-8 CIP 1988

John Wain: A Bibliography
by David Gerard
ISBN 0-88736-103-X CIP 1988

The Making of the Shelley Myth:
An Annotated Bibliography of Criticism of
P.B. Shelley, 1822-1860
by Karsten Klejs Engelberg
ISBN 0-88736-298-2 CIP 1988

PKD: A Philip K. Dick Bibliography,
Revised Edition
by Daniel J. H. Levack and Steven Owen
Godersky
ISBN 0-88736-096-3 CIP 1988

Dune Master: A Frank Herbert
Bibliography
by Daniel J. H. Levack and Mark Willard
ISBN 0-88736-099-8 CIP 1988

Gothic Fiction: A Master List of
Twentieth Century Criticism
and Research
by Frederick S. Frank
ISBN 0-88736-218-4 CIP 1988

The Bibliography of Contemporary
American Fiction, 1945-1988:
An Annotated Checklist
by William McPheron and
Jocelyn Sheppard
ISBN 0-88736-167-6 CIP 1989

Robinson Crusoe: An Annotated
Checklist of English Language Editions,
1719-1985
by Robert Lovett
ISBN 0-88736-058-0 CIP forthcoming

Donald Davie: A Descriptive Bibliography
by Stuart Wright
ISBN 0-88736-059-9 CIP forthcoming

John Ciardi: A Descriptive Bibliography
by Charles C. Lovett and
Stephanie B. Lovett
ISBN 0-88736-056-4 CIP forthcoming

Lewis Carroll's Alice: An Annotated
Checklist of Editions in English
by Charles C. Lovett and
Stephanie B. Lovett
ISBN 0-88736-166-8 CIP forthcoming

Robert Lowell: A Descriptive
Bibliography
by Stephen Gould Axelrod
ISBN 0-88736-227-3 CIP forthcoming

James Tate: A Descriptive Bibliography
by Gene DeGruson
ISBN 0-88736-229-X CIP forthcoming

Richard Eberhart: A Descriptive
Bibliography, 1921-1987
by Stuart Wright
ISBN 0-88736-346-6 CIP 1989

Clifford Odets: An Annotated
Bibliography, 1935-1989
by Robert Cooperman
ISBN 0-88736-326-1 CIP 1989

CLIFFORD ODETS

An Annotated Bibliography

1935-1989

Robert Cooperman

Meckler

Westport • London

Library of Congress Cataloging-in-Publication Data

Cooperman, Robert.
    Clifford Odets : an annotated bibliography,
1935-1989.

    Includes index.
    1. Odets, Clifford, 1906-1963--Bibliography.
I. Title
Z8641 . 13 . C66 1990   016.812 ' 52   88-27299
[PS3529.D46]
ISBN 0-88736-326-1 (alk. paper)

British Library Cataloguing in Publication Data

Cooperman, Robert
    Clifford Odets: an annotated bibliography,
    1935-1989.
    1. Drama in English. American writers. Odets,
    Clifford, 1906-1963 -- Bibliographies
    I. Title
    016 . 812 ' 54

    ISBN 0-88736-326-1

Meckler Corporation, 11 Ferry Lane West, Westport, CT 06880.
Meckler Ltd., Grosvenor Gardens House, Grosvenor Gardens,
  London SW1W 0BS, U.K.

Printed on acid free paper.
Printed in the United States of America.

Contents

Clifford Odets (Photographed by Alfredo Valente; Courtesy of Walt Odets)

Acknowledgments

I am very much indebted to Professor Margaret Loftus Ranald of Queens College, CUNY, for guidance, suggestions, and, above all, the recommendation that I pursue publication of this material. Of no lesser importance has been the help of Professor Charles A. Carpenter of SUNY Binghamton who was gracious enough to read the original manuscript. Professor Carpenter offered a great many guidelines for its improvement, and made himself available to answer a multitude of questions.

Special thanks are due to Selma Luttinger of the Robert A. Freedman Dramatic Agency for providing valuable and up-to-date information, and for putting me in communication with Walt Odets. Deep gratitude is also extended to Walt Odets for his invaluable help in obtaining information concerning his father's manuscripts, papers, and diaries. Mr. Odets also graciously provided the fine portrait of his father used in this book.

A debt is owed to Professor Michael J. Mendelsohn of the University of Tampa for his help in obtaining a copy of his book, and for his careful consideration of a troublesome question concerning a transcontinental title change in Odets' play The Country Girl. Thanks are also due to Margaret Brenman-Gibson for pondering this question. Special thanks go to Virginia Rowe, Odets' last secretary, for conducting a substantial amount of research in order to answer this aforementioned puzzlement, providing, in turn, a great deal of important background material on both The Country Girl and The Big Knife. Finally, gratitude is extended to Sam Wanamaker for furnishing the final answer to this controversy, as well as other valuable information.

Others who graciously furnished information and/or assistance are: Dorothy Swerdlove of the New York Public Library at Lincoln Center, Ed Limato and Chris Andrews of International Creative Management, Kimberly Padula of Harper and Row, Frances Bartky, Jean Devlin, Frank Gaffney, Walt Bode of Grove Press, Anthony Abbott of the Meckler Corporation, and, especially, Sandra Bartky, for her help, faith, and love.

Robert Cooperman
New York, 1989

Chronology

1906	Born in Philadelphia on July 18 to Pearl Geisinger Odets and Louis Odets.
1910	Sister Genevieve born.
1912	Family moves to New York City after previous moves to the Bronx and again to Philadelphia.
1916	Sister Florence born.
1921	Enters Morris High School. Acts in school plays. Leaves school in 1923.
1924-1929	Acts with several theatre companies. Works as a disc jockey in New York and Philadelphia. Writes radio play, At the Waterline, which is ultimately produced. Understudies Spencer Tracy in the Broadway production of Conflict.
1930	Acts with the Theatre Guild. Partakes in early meetings with the Group Theatre. Begins writing short stories and novels.

1931	Becomes charter member of the newly-formed Group Theatre; acts in minor roles. Turns attention to playwriting.
1932	Writes I Got the Blues which will eventually become Awake and Sing! Continues acting and directing.
1933	Second act of Awake and Sing! presented by the Group Theatre.
1934	Begins work on Paradise Lost. Writes Waiting for Lefty which wins play contest sponsored by New Theatre magazine. Group Theatre accepts Awake and Sing! for production.
January 1935	Benefit performance of Waiting for Lefty makes Odets an overnight sensation.
February	Awake and Sing! opens on Broadway at the Belasco Theatre.
March	Waiting for Lefty and Till the Day I Die open at the Longacre Theatre. Lefty is awarded the George Pierce Baker Drama Cup, Yale University.
April	Three Plays By Clifford Odets published by Covici-Friede.
May	Death of Pearl Geisinger Odets.

July	Leads delegation to Cuba to protest American interests there. Arrested and deported.
December	Paradise Lost opens at the Longacre Theatre.
1936	Travels to Hollywood. Meets Louise Rainer. Writes screenplay The General Died at Dawn. Monologue, I Can't Sleep, published in New Theatre magazine.
1937	Marries Louise Rainer in Los Angeles. Writes several unproduced screenplays and The Silent Partner before returning to New York. Golden Boy opens at the Belasco Theatre.
1938	Separation and reconciliation with Rainer. Rocket to the Moon opens at the Belasco Theatre.
1939	Separates from Rainer. Six Plays of Clifford Odets published by Random House.
1940	Night Music opens at the Broadhurst Theatre. Writes screenplay for Night Music in Hollywood which is never produced.
1941	Withdraws from the Group Theatre which disbands soon after. Clash By Night

	opens at the Belasco Theatre. Divorces Louise Rainer.
1942	Adapts Simonov's The Russian People for the stage which is produced by the Theatre Guild. Writes various unproduced screenplays in Hollywood.
1943	Marries Bette Grayson. Writes screenplay for None But the Lonely Heart and directs film.
1944	Writes various unproduced screenplays in Hollywood.
1945	Daughter Nora born.
1946	Screenplay for Deadline at Dawn produced by RKO.
1947	Son Walt born. Named a Communist by the House Un-American Activities Committee. Screenplay for Humoresque produced by Warner Brothers.
1949	The Big Knife opens at the National Theatre.
1950	The Country Girl opens at the Lyceum Theatre.
1951	Divorced from Bette Grayson.
1952	Questioned by the House Un-American Activities Committee.

1954	Death of Bette Grayson. Moves to Hollywood with children. <u>The Flowering Peach</u> opens at the Belasco Theatre.
1957	Screenplay for <u>The Sweet Smell of Success</u> produced by United Artists.
1959	Screenplay for <u>The Story on Page One</u> produced by 20th Century-Fox.
1960	Screenplay for <u>Wild in the Country</u> produced by 20th Century-Fox.
1961	Receives award from the American Academy of Arts and Letters.
1963	Signs with NBC as script supervisor and story editor for <u>The Richard Boone Show</u>. Writes three teleplays, two of which are aired. Dies on August 14 of cancer.

Part One:
Bibliographic Essay

Introduction

Scholarship on Clifford Odets (1906-1963) peaked sometime in the late 1930's and slowly dissipated until his death. The years immediately following Odets' death did not bring about any great revival or interest, although, as expected, more articles did appear -- mostly eulogies and remembrances. Criticism over the past two decades has, for the most part, devaluated the Odets canon, placing it within the framework of a historical movement, valuable only in retrospect. Although he also wrote film scripts and articles, his plays have earned the great majority of scholarly attention from 1935-1989. Odets is now considered a product of a particular era in American history; a typical representative of a brief, yet productive moment in time. With some very recent exceptions, he is rarely mentioned as an important contributor to twentieth-century drama by post-1970 scholars.

This essay, an overview of the major trends in Odets

scholarship, is divided into categories which have their counterpart in the bibliography. Each will offer the best general sources for information to be found under that particular category.

Since no comprehensive bibliographical study of Clifford Odets exists before the present attempt, research was prepared by perusing the various standard bibliographical texts in American literature and/or drama, and the full-length studies of Odets. Helpful sources include: Lewis Leary's Articles On American Literature 1900-1950 (1954. Suppls: 1950-1967, 1968-1975); American Drama Criticism, compiled by Floyd E. Eddleman (1979); and Helen Palmer and Jane Dyson's American Drama Criticism: Interpretations 1890-1965 (1967). Sources of the greatest value after the publication of this bibliography, of course, will be those which are constantly updated. One such source is Modern Drama which publishes an annual bibliography in every June issue. These bibliographies supplement Charles A. Carpenter's Modern Drama. Scholarship and Criticism 1966-1980: An International Bibliography (1981), a major source for information in this bibliography. Additional sources which may be of value to future Odets research include the MLA International Bibliography, which provides a new supplement each year, and the Annual Bibliography of English Language and Literature, which also publishes a yearly volume.

Manuscripts

The subject of Odets manuscripts is indeed a troubling one. Quite a few libraries claim to have Odets manuscripts, yet no scholar has ever attempted to discover precisely which manuscripts they own. Unless reported in a catalogue (like those of the Library of Congress or the New York Public Library, at Lincoln Center), researchers must be content with the superficial knowledge that certain unnamed manuscripts are available at specific institutions. Even more frustrating is the fact that while typescripts of the published plays are easy enough to locate (New York Public has most of them), manuscripts for unpublished works are difficult to track down.

The collection at the New York Public is unquestionably the richest depository of Odets material in the country. This Literary Estate of Clifford Odets, mentioned frequently by Margaret Brenman-Gibson in <u>Clifford Odets: American Playwright</u>, contains an enormous amount of unpublished material, most of it never before scrutinized by researchers. The Estate is looked after by Odets' son, Walt, who has been inventorying its contents and donating them to the New York Public Library at Lincoln Center since 1981. A substantial amount of material can now be found at the New York Public, though some of it has yet to be inventoried.

Items to be found there as of 1988 include:

<u>PUBLISHED PLAYS</u> - may include notes and/or revisions.

1. <u>Awake and Sing!</u> - Early scripts entitled "I Got The
   Blues"; act 3 of "I Got The Blues"; 1st or 2nd drafts.

2. <u>The Big Knife</u> - Early drafts known as "A Winter Journey";
   various other drafts; film treatment after publication
   of play.

3. <u>Clash by Night</u> - 1st through 6th drafts including name
   change: "Can You Take It"; copy of contract between
   Odets and Wald-Krasma Productions to produce play.

4. <u>The Country Girl</u> - Early draft; 3rd and 4th drafts;
   "Final, As Being Played" version.

5. <u>The Flowering Peach</u> - Manuscript copy.

6. <u>Golden Boy</u> - Original materials entitled "Golden Gloves";
   manuscript copy.

7. <u>I Can't Sleep</u> - Manuscript copy.

8. <u>Paradise Lost</u> - Carbon copy of script; 3rd draft (differs
   from final version); typescript.

9. <u>Rocket to the Moon</u> - Manuscript copy.

10. <u>The Silent Partner</u> - Early script; 2nd draft; working
    script.

11. <u>Waiting for Lefty</u> - Copy in Hebrew; "Revised script" with
    significant differences from the published versions;

French version of play; radio adaptation by Victor E.
Smith.

UNPUBLISHED SCRIPTS/SCREENPLAYS - may include revisions or
notes. One copy unless otherwise noted.

1. The Cuban Play (1935-38. A.k.a. "The Law of Flight") - two
     drafts; one copy.
2. Gettysburg (1937. Screenplay shelved by Paramount).
3. Mother's Day (1936. By Odets and Elia Kazan under
     pseudonyms).
4. 910 Eden Street (1931).
5. Three Sisters (1931. Adaptation of Chekhov play).
6. Victory (A.k.a. "Brant Play," "Beethoven Play").

RADIO SCRIPTS

1. At The Waterline (1926) - First produced by WFBH, New
     York.

DIARIES/JOURNALS

For the years: 1924, 1926, 1932, 1940 (now published. See
"Journals and Diaries"), 1951, 1952, 1953, 1955, 1958, 1961,
1962, 1963.

SHORT STORIES - unpublished, originals, only known copies.
All with notes.

1. "A Faint Smile." - 16 pp.

2. "My Friend The Greek." - 1 p.

3. "Olive Weston." (1930-31) - 3 pp.

4. "One Hot Night." (1930-31) - 16 pp.

5. "School Incident." (1926-28) - 7 pp.

6. "Small Birds." (1928-29) - 5 pp.

7. "Small Birds Fly Against The Wind." - 7 pp. Title
   crossed out.

8. "The Story of Pat Lawrence As It Happened." - 13 pp.

9. "The Violinist." (1930 or 1931) - 18 pp.

10. Two untitled pieces.

MISCELLANEOUS ITEMS

1. Photos. - Family, other subjects.

2. Paintings by Odets.

3. Letters, telegrams.

4. Notes, story ideas.

5. Poems (1932).

6. Film (16mm) - 30 minutes of television interview entitled
   Sum and Substance. Last interview with Odets. Herman
   Harvey, interviewer. (Feb. 3, 1963).

7. Various articles and speeches, most fully annotated in "Articles By Odets."

SOLD AT AUCTION - items which were at one time a part of this collection but have been sold at auction.

1. Typescript of The Big Knife.
2. Carbon copy of RKO contract for Odets to serve as director of None But the Lonely Heart.
3. Carbon copy of RKO contract for Odets to produce screen adaptation of None But the Lonely Heart.
4. Carbon copy of RKO contract for Odets to serve as writer for screen adaptation of A Tree Grows in Brooklyn.

According to Gerald Weales, the Lincoln Center collection holds the unpublished "Castles in Spain" (Weales, Odets: Playwright 197). The Theatre Collection also holds promptbooks for Clash by Night and Rocket to the Moon. The Berg Collection of English and American Literature holds a signed and dated presentation copy of The Big Knife and a typescript of Odets' adaptation of The Russian People. Also in the Berg Collection are: the George Cram Cook Library Collection which includes playbills bearing Odets' name as an actor; the papers of stage actress Hortense Alden which includes correspondence from Odets along with four unnamed, signed and dated typescripts; the files of the American Play Company including correspondence, forms, and statements concerning Odets; and the New Theatre League Collection which includes Odets' correspondence with Ben Irwin (the League's executive secretary) and Alice Hamburger Evans (of the Play Department).

The Library of Congress has a typescript of "I Got The Blues" (which became Awake and Sing!, "The Silent Partner," "The Cuban Play," and "Sarah Bernhardt" (all unpublished, the latter two unproduced) (Weales, Playwright 197). Also, the Manuscript Division holds the papers of playwright, author, and copyright specialist George Middleton which includes correspondence with Odets.

Ohio State University owns a mimeographed script of The Big Knife. A carbon-copy typescript of the acting version of The Russian People is available at the Beinecke Rare Book and Manuscript Library at Yale University. The Beinecke also has various Odets letters.

A typed copy of The Flowering Peach (along with letters and documents) can be found at the Manuscript Collection at the Butler Library, Columbia University. This contradicts Harold Cantor's claim that he alone owns the typescript of Peach. Cantor also claims that the play was never published (214); however, both Brandt & Brandt and the Dramatists Play Service had published acting editions of Peach in 1954. Perhaps Cantor does not consider an acting edition to be a published edition. Shuman also draws this conclusion, noting that the play is available only in typescript (Odets 152).

Yet, he credits the Dramatists Play Service publication of the play as an edition, as he does for The Country Girl. At any rate, Cantor apparently was unaware at the time (1978) that Columbia owns a typescript, as does the previously mentioned New York Public Library.

According to American Literary Manuscripts (2nd. ed. 1977), the Mugar Memorial Library at Boston University owns a manuscript as well as letters and other memorabilia. However, according to Charlie Niles, Reference Librarian at the Mugar Library, no manuscript is to be found in the library. He speculated that either the editors of ALM may have misinterpreted the Library's holdings, or that the donor of the Odets material may have taken the manuscript back when he or she withdrew some material (for reasons Mr. Niles could not explain). Mr. Niles did reveal that the Library owns the papers of Irene Mayer Selznick, which include letters to and from Odets, autographed photos, and various contracts signed by Odets.

Letters, correspondence, and other materials of or about Odets can be found at numerous libraries around the country in the following collections: The Walter Conrad Arensberg Collection at the Francis Bacon Library, Claremont, California; the John Steinbeck letters at the University of Virginia Library; The Random House Collection (Records, 1925-68) at Columbia University; the Christopher Darlington Morley letters at Haverford College Library (Odets correspondence

from 1928); and The John Gassner Collection at the
Hoblitzelle Theatre Arts Library in Austin, Texas. Other
libraries with Odets holdings include: University of
California Research Library, LA; Bancroft Library, University
of California, Berkeley; Newberry Library, Chicago; Delyte W.
Morris Library, Southern Illinois University; Lilly Library,
Indiana University; Houghton Library, Harvard University; the
American Jewish Historical Society; University of Michigan;
FDR Library; John M. Olin Library, Cornell University; Fales
Library, New York University; Pack Memorial Public Library,
University of Oklahoma; Fred Lewis Pattee Library, Penn State
University; Charles Patterson Van Pelt Library, University of
Pennsylvania; Humanities Research Center, University of
Texas; University of Wyoming, Archive of Contemporary
History.

Researchers are to be advised that all inquiries for the
use of Odets material should be addressed to his literary
representatives, the Robert A. Freedman Dramatic Agency,
Inc., 1501 Broadway, Suite 2310, New York, NY 10036.

TEXTS

To date, there are no critical editions of Odets' plays.
As far as can be ascertained, they have been published as
performed (except for Waiting for Lefty).

The standard text for most of Clifford Odets' plays is
the Random House publication of Six Plays of Clifford Odets

(1939; Grove Press, 1979). This edition includes <u>Waiting for Lefty</u>, <u>Awake and Sing!</u>, <u>Till the Day I Die</u>, <u>Paradise Lost</u>, <u>Golden Boy</u>, and <u>Rocket to the Moon</u>. The version of <u>Waiting for Lefty</u> included in this edition does not contain "The Young Actor" scene, which was performed in the original Group Theatre production of 1935, but which Odets excluded before publication. It is said that Odets removed this scene because it is blatantly Marxist; a receptionist gives the actor some money to buy <u>The Communist Manifesto</u>. Having joined and left the Communist party by 1939, Odets was obviously sensitive about being labeled a member of any one particular political group. "The Young Actor" scene can be found in other anthologies; its inclusion often causes that version of <u>Lefty</u> to be called a "complete" version. One such anthology is <u>Representative American Plays</u> (1952 -- full documentation in bibliography). <u>Waiting for Lefty</u> has also been published, complete, by V. Gollancz in London (1938). These editions were known as "Left Book Club Editions" and were not for sale to the general public.

Random House has also published editions of <u>The Big Knife</u> (1946, 1949), <u>Clash by Night</u> (1942), and <u>Night Music</u> (1940). Other editions and/or publishers are listed in the bibliography (<u>see</u> "The Published Works of Clifford Odets").

An Odets play entitled <u>A Winter Journey</u> may cause some confusion for researchers. This title appears in conjunction with two published plays, <u>The Big Knife</u> and <u>The Country Girl</u>.

A Winter Journey first appears as the working title of The Big Knife, although Odets also considered My Sins as the play's title. He even attempted to copyright the play as A Winter Journey in September of 1948, but his application was refused due to insufficient funds. However, he titled the play's fourth draft The Big Knife, and this, of course, became the final, copyrighted title of the play. In 1952, a London production of The Country Girl underwent a title change. It became A Winter Journey (or, more correctly, Winter Journey) and starred Michael Redgrave and Sam Wanamaker (who also served as director and co-producer). Kenneth Tynan in Curtains reviews this production and notes the title change (see Curtains in "Critical Studies: Individual Plays" - The Country Girl). Odets considered The Actor and No Pity as possible titles for The Country Girl, but there is no evidence that he considered A Winter Journey as a possible title. The title change is therefore a bit of a puzzlement. The answer, however, is quite simple: when Odets brought The Country Girl to London in 1952, there was a very popular musical comedy of the same name running there. To avoid confusion, Odets suggested Winter Journey to Wanamaker and others. No changes were made in the script as a result of the change in title. In the bibliography, all commentary on Winter Journey will be included under those for The Country Girl.

The following categories are those which are fully annotated in the bibliography, in the order in which they appear.

ARTICLES BY ODETS

While best remembered as a playwright, Clifford Odets was often a contributor to The New York Times as a commentator on playwriting and Hollywood screenwriting (often defending his decision to move to Hollywood). Odets also contributed remembrances of Thomas Wolfe and John Garfield. A very important article credited to Odets in the September 1966 issue of Harper's entitled "How A Playwright Triumphs" provides various insights into many facets of the playwright's life. Although any one of the above-mentioned sources would be useful as biographical material (especially the Harper's piece), they are placed in a separate section due to the fact that they all bear Odets' name as author.

JOURNALS AND DIARIES

The only entry in this section is the recently published 1940 journal entitled The Time Is Ripe. Odets wrote this, his only journal, with possible publication in mind. An evaluation of this journal can be found in Gabriel Miller's Clifford Odets (1989) which is annotated in the "Critical Studies: General" section of the bibliography. To date, his diaries, most of which can be found at the New York Public Library at Lincoln Center, have not been published.

BIOGRAPHICAL MATERIALS

Until 1981, the full-length studies of Clifford Odets
have been critical studies, that is, evaluations of the Odets
canon. Scholars apparently had found little occasion to
chronicle the man's life in any detail. Robert Baird
Shuman's Clifford Odets is a typical example; his
biographical details are limited to a non-elaborate overview,
with some important dates and events briefly highlighted.
The rest of his book is basically a critical study of Odets'
plays.

In 1963, Margaret Brenman-Gibson began the enormous task
of compiling Odets' letters, diaries, notebooks, and family
information in order to develop the first full-length
biography of the playwright (Preface xiv). In 1981, the
first volume of her work was published, a 750-page book which
spans the years 1906 through 1940. The second volume will
cover the rest of Odets' life. This study, while of course
indispensable, suffers from an over-detailing of
psychological data and its excessive length renders it
unappealing, especially since it does not cover Odets' entire
life span. For a critique of the book, the reader should
consult Saul Maloff's "The Thirties and Clifford Who?" (1982)
("Critical Studies: General" in bibliography). This book
does, however, attempt to sort out the specific details of
Odets' life, a tedious task since many have found that Odets'

own recollections are not to be trusted.

Other good sources for biographical material include Harold Clurman's The Fervent Years (the Group Theatre years only) and All People Are Famous (The Fervent Years listed in "Critical Studies: Politics and the Group Theatre" section). Both provide insightful, first-hand (although not totally unbiased) observations. Burns Mantle's Contemporary American Playwrights (1939) contains some valuable information about Odets' early life and career as an actor. Similar information can be found in John McCarten's "Revolution's Number One Boy" from 1938. Both are useful and reliable sources for information concerning Odets' early life and background, and, there is much material regarding Odets' hobbies, habits, and idiosyncrasies.

Excellent insights into Odets' state of mind in the years just prior to his death can be found in Michael J. Mendelsohn's "Odets At Center Stage," an interview from 1961 (although not printed until 1963). In this interview, Odets offers views on everything from contemporary theatre to television. In addition, this interview affords the researcher some character study not yet available from Margaret Brenman-Gibson. Lesser sources of biographical material include accounts from close friends, eulogies, and newspaper stories about Odets (some not involving playwriting).

CRITICAL STUDIES: GENERAL

This section of the bibliography is divided into the following four periods: "1935-1940," "1941-1950," "1951-1963," and "1964-Present." The intention is to provide the reader with a chronological overview of the changes in attitude towards Odets within these periods. One can sense the high praise of the first period, the fading interest of the second period, the slight resurgence of interest, hope for a comeback, and a mellowing of attitude (which some have attributed to a maturity on Odets' part) in the third period, and the disappointment at Odets' supposed failure to live up to his past in the last period. Also, the scholarly reassessment of Odets' work from 1964 to 1989 can be traced: a definite move away from any serious consideration of his entire canon (despite the full-length studies) towards a more specific analysis of particular themes and motifs typical of 1930's drama.

To date, there are six full-length critical studies of Clifford Odets, all but one written at least five years after his death. It is debatable whether or not this is to be viewed as a sudden interest in Odets specifically or merely an interest in the drama of the Thirties. In any case, the one full-length study prior to Odets' death is R. Baird Shuman's Clifford Odets (1962). Shuman's work stresses the family element in the plays and the "falseness" Odets found in society and human existence (146). Although Shuman has done a great deal of work on Odets since the publication of his book, his many errors (as a number of scholars have pointed out) must make his scholarship suspect. The next major study is Edward Murray's <u>Clifford Odets: The Thirties and After</u> (1968). Murray argues that previous criticism has not done justice to Odets; the later plays compare favorably with the earlier ones. Murray also tries to downplay the critical notion that Odets' characters are directly autobiographical. In 1969, Michael J. Mendelsohn offered <u>Clifford Odets: Humane Dramatist</u>. It is not at all surprising that Mendelsohn would publish such a study; his well-known interview with Odets and his numerous articles about the playwright surely deserve full-length recognition. This book stresses the humanitarian aspects of Odets' work and downplays the radicalism so often attributed to him. In addition, Mendelsohn offers the finest assessment of Odets' Hollywood and television career to date. Gerald Weales, another frequent Odets researcher, published <u>Clifford Odets: Playwright</u> in 1971. Weales is particularly hostile to the three previous full-length studies, noting Shuman's errors in particular. This book stresses the theme of homelessness and alienation in Odets' work, as well as his hope and optimism for humanity. Weales attempts to present a well-rounded view of both Odets the man and Odets the playwright, and by doing so, makes this a valuable book for biographical materials. In 1978, Harold Cantor offered an expanded version of his 1975

dissertation entitled Clifford Odets: Playwright-Poet.
Cantor approaches the Odets canon by themes and motifs rather
than play by play. In this way he shows Odets' work to be
homogeneous and not just a series of individual plays. The
latest published study is Gabriel Miller's Clifford Odets
(1989). Miller, like Cantor, refrains from the chronological
approach, opting instead to offer discussions on the use of
romance, melodrama, and tragedy in Odets' plays. In
addition, a new book by William W. Demastes (Greenwood Press,
publisher) will provide annotated entries on the performance
aspects of Odets' work, as well as biographical information.
Demastes' work is due to appear sometime in 1990.

All remaining commentary on Odets is to be found in
periodicals and/or lengthy reviews in books. Among the best
are John Gassner's study of allegorizing in Odets' work in
"The Long Journey of a Talent" (1949), Malcolm Goldstein's
"The Playwrights of the 1930's" (Chapter 3 of Alan S.
Downer's The American Theater Today [1967]) in which
Goldstein lends a sobering note to the usual tide of euphoric
Odets criticism, and Harold Clurman's The Naked Image (1958)
in which Clurman argues that the nature of Odets' work was a
self-portrayal and a confession of sorts. Also of value
because of its originality is W. David Sievers' Freud on
Broadway (1955) which offers a psychological study of Odets'
work. Malcolm Goldstein explores similar avenues in "Body
and Soul on Broadway" (1965), although not nearly in as much

detail as Sievers. In many ways, Sievers' work is the
predecessor to Margaret Brenman Gibson's psychological
interpretation.

In general, critical response to Odets' work has shown a
gradual disappointment on the part of scholars who expected
so much of the man after Waiting for Lefty and Awake and
Sing!. Most scholars over the past 20 years have
acknowledged that Odets was unable to equal or surpass the
artistic merits that he achieved with these first two plays.
A typical example of the early, high expectations, is Joseph
Wood Krutch's The American Drama Since 1918 (1939). Krutch
incorrectly predicts a constant artistic improvement by
Odets. Also, Stark Young's "New Talents" (1935) ironically
ponders the idea that it would be great fun indeed if he were
the only critic to see Odets as a major, lasting talent. For
particularly hostile views, see anything by George Jean
Nathan (also of interest is Odets' rather vehement response
to Nathan's criticisms in Mendelsohn's "Odets At Center
Stage"). A most level-headed view is sounded by Catherine
Hughes' "Odets: The Price of Success" (1963). Hughes notes
the unfairness involved in judging Odets' later work against
his early successes. Recent criticism has attempted to find
a place for Odets within the history of twentieth-century
American drama. Studies such as Ruby Cohn and Bernard F.
Dukore's Twentieth Century Drama: England, Ireland, and the
United States (1966) and C. W. E. Bigsby's A Critical

Introduction to Twentieth-Century American Drama (1982) note certain aspects of Odets' dramaturgy (visionary qualities, use of agit-prop, etc.), but fail to find any major importance or lasting value in his work.

Major trends often noticed by critics include Odets' use of vivid and electrifying dialogue. John Gassner in Masters of the Drama (1940) presents a well-rounded consensus of the positive and negative aspects of Odets' dialogue. Ruby Cohn in Dialogue In American Drama (1971) focuses on the Jewishness of Odets' phrasing. Although no lengthy studies treat this aspect of Odets, almost all critical analyses mention it.

Odets' work is often compared with that of Russian playwright Anton Chekhov in terms of dramatic structure and technique. John Mason Brown's Dramatis Personae (1963) provides a good listing of Chekhovian characteristics and their application to Odets (72). A better study is Charles W. Meister's "Comparative Drama: Chekhov, Shaw, Odets" (1950), which details the Chekhovian techniques and directly applies them to Odets' work. Also of much value is Gabriel Miller's Clifford Odets (1989) which devotes an entire chapter to the Chekhov question.

Harold Clurman appears to be the one critic who disagrees with the Chekhov parallel. In The Naked Image (1958), he sees very little Chekhovian influence (see also "Three Introductions" by Clurman in "Critical Studies:

Individual Plays" - <u>Awake and Sing!</u>). Of course, Clurman's version may be apocryphal owing to his tendency to "protect" the best interests of his close friend. Odets himself was known to dismiss the Chekhov parallel, preferring Victor Hugo as a genuine influence (<u>see also</u> "Odets At Center Stage" [Mendelsohn] in "Biographical Materials"). However, Odets was known to be unreliable. All references to Chekhov are noted in the annotations.

Another trend in Odets scholarship focuses on his constant use of Jewish characters, dialogue, dialect, and themes. Although this aspect of Odets' dramaturgy was briefly noticed by Grenville Vernon in 1938, and again by Robert S. Warshow in 1946, it was not until 1966 that it was studied in any great detail. In that year, Gerald W. Haslam fully characterized and described the "Yiddish-English" spoken by Odets' characters ("Odets' Use of Yiddish-English in <u>Awake and Sing!</u>"). Robert Baird Shuman discussed the effect of a Jewish home on Odets in "Clifford Odets: A Playwright and His Jewish Background" (1972). Similar facts are discussed in Shuman's "Clifford Odets and the Jewish Context" from 1983. By contrast, Grenville Vernon's "Clifford Odets" (1938) observes that Jewishness is a severe limitation on Odets' playwriting ability (up to 1938).

CRITICAL STUDIES: INDIVIDUAL PLAYS

This section is divided by play in alphabetical order.

Researchers should note that it lists only those sources which deal directly, or mostly, with a particular play, not those found in any one of the previously mentioned full-length critical studies. However, the full-length studies should certainly be consulted for additional information on any given play.

By far the most consistent and interesting reviews on individual plays are provided by Brooks Atkinson, drama critic for the New York Times from 1926 to 1960. Atkinson reviewed every play thoroughly in his column. Other reviewers of interest include John Mason Brown (in various books, periodicals, and newspapers), Harold Clurman (also in various publications), and Edith Isaacs of Theatre Arts.

CRITICAL STUDIES: POLITICS AND THE GROUP THEATRE

Throughout his career, Clifford Odets was artistically linked to the Group Theatre, even years after it disbanded in 1941. It was as a member of the Group that Odets became an overnight sensation; Waiting for Lefty and Awake and Sing! gave birth to both Odets as a playwright, and to the Group Theatre as a theatrical movement. Many have pointed out just how dependent Odets was on the Group and the Group on Odets.

Although not necessarily a politically motivated ensemble, the Group became known as a forum for leftist dramatic material after Waiting for Lefty (the fact is that the group had been producing the plays of Marxist John Howard Lawson for years prior to Lefty). Because of the undeniable socialist/Marxist statement made by both Waiting for Lefty and Awake and Sing!, Clifford Odets became identified with many of the political and/or class-conscious literary movements of the 1930's: socialist, Marxist, Communist, proletarian, middle-class, etc., and his work became the representative literature of the era. One look at his present-day standing shows that, despite his later non-political plays, he was unable to transcend this reputation.

The definitive source on the Group Theatre is Harold Clurman's The Fervent Years (1945, reprinted 1975). Only the events and plays of Odets' Group Theatre years (1935-1940; from Lefty to Night Music) are discussed.

Although nothing compares to Clurman's indispensable work, there are some other good studies concerning the Group Theatre. Mordecai Gorelik, a set designer for the Group, provides some good observations in New Theatres For Old (1940). For a brief, undetailed history of the Group and its reasons for existence, see Gerald Weales' "The Group Theatre and Its Plays" (1967). The December 1976 issue of the Educational Theatre Journal (Helen Krich Chinoy, ed.) is devoted entirely to the Group Theatre with a special section on Odets.

Studies on the politics of the 1930's and their direct influence on Odets include Malcolm Goldstein's "Clifford

Odets and the Found Generation" (1965) and The Political
Stage (1974). Gerald Rabkin's Drama and Commitment (1964) is
another fine study which highlights the need of Depression
audiences for a playwright like Odets.

HOUSE UN-AMERICAN ACTIVITIES COMMITTEE

In 1952, Clifford Odets testified before a House
committee investigating un-American activities. His
testimony proved to be uneventful as he cooperated fully with
the Committee members. As a result of his rather non-
confrontational admissions, Odets' testimony has been of
little interest to scholars. Saul Maloff was personally
offended by Odets' cooperation with the Government (see
Maloff in "Critical Studies: General"), but his views are of
little value to those interested in the HUAC. A better
source is Eric Bentley's Thirty Years of Treason (1971) which
includes excerpts (some quite lengthy) from Odets' testimony.
Also, there are various publications provided by the
Government which include excerpts and information from the
Odets testimony. These publications are listed in the
bibliography.

DISSERTATIONS

To date, there are eleven doctoral dissertations about
Odets, issued in 1961, 1962, 1963, two in 1964, 1970, 1974,
1975, 1980, 1981, and 1986. This shows a sudden interest in

Odets in the years just prior to, and directly after, his death. Significantly, interest seems to have waned after 1964, despite some attention in the 1970's and 1980's. Also of note is the fact that three of these dissertations have become full-length studies: Shuman (1961), Mendelsohn (1962), and Cantor (1975). In general, these dissertations show an interest in praising Odets' achievements and downplaying the genre labels (social protest, politics, etc.) that have become associated with him. Odets' influence on Arthur Miller has also become an oft-noted dissertation topic.

THE FUTURE OF ODETS SCHOLARSHIP

Owing to the general lack of interest in Clifford Odets over the past 20 years, the future of Odets scholarship appears to be in jeopardy. Yet, there may be a resurgence of interest on the horizon. The recent work by Gabriel Miller, the published journal of 1940, and the soon-to-be published performance study by William Demastes may be an indication of some earnest scholarly consideration of Odets' work. Time will tell whether this is a true revival, or simply another brief, but uninspired examination.

Still, there is work to be done, if only for the sake of American theatrical studies. Odets' manuscripts, especially those of the unpublished plays, need to be located and studied so that the full output of the man can be realized. The Chekhov influence needs to be more fully researched and

applied to the entire Odets canon, not just <u>Awake and Sing!</u>
and <u>Paradise Lost</u>. A full-length study on this topic should
be considered. A more accessible biography, with less of an
emphasis on psychological detail, might also be a
possibility.

The publication of Odets' 1940 journal (<u>see also</u>
"Journals and Diaries") has opened up a new field of study
different from the usual play-by-play, themes-and-motifs
analysis. The diaries found at the New York Public Library
at Lincoln Center (<u>see also</u> "Manuscripts") may provide
insights into Odets' mind which have heretofore been
overlooked. Margaret Brenman-Gibson's <u>Clifford Odets:</u>
<u>American Playwright</u> has made good use of the diaries for this
purpose. Also, the numerous short stories and poems to be
found at the New York Public Library at Lincoln Center are
certainly worth some attention.

Odets' Hollywood years are another area that should be
looked into. There is precious little information concerning
his life at the movie studios. Besides formal critiques of
his films, it would be very interesting to discover exactly
for which films he was a "ghost writer." These films could
then be reviewed in order to reveal any "Odetsisms" that may
still exist.

There is now the hope that Odets will not join the ranks
of the forgotten, and sufficient material is available to
ensure that he does not. The aforementioned new works have

the potential to elevate Odets to a new level of prominence. Ironically, they may finally allow his work to emerge from the shadow of the word "promising" which haunted him throughout his creative life.

Part Two:
Published Works
of
Clifford Odets

1. <u>Awake and Sing!</u>

   a. New York: Covici-Friede, 1935.

   b. New York: Random House, 1935.

2. <u>The Big Knife</u>

   a. New York: Random House, 1946. Reprinted 1949.

   b. New York: Dramatists Play Service, 1949. Reprinted 1963.

3. <u>Clash by Night</u>

   a. New York: Random House, 1942.

4. <u>The Country Girl</u>

   a. New York: Dramatists Play Service, 1951.

   b. New York: Viking Press, 1951.

5. <u>The Flowering Peach</u>

   a. New York: Brandt and Brandt Dramatic Dept., 1954.

   b. New York: Dramatists Play Service, 1954.

6. <u>Golden Boy</u>

   a. New York: Dramatists Play Service, 1937.

b. New York: Random House, 1937.

c. London: V. Gollancz, 1938.

d. New York: The Modern Library, 1939.

7. I Can't Sleep

a. New Theatre and Film 3 (Feb. 1936): 8-9.

8. Night Music

a. New York: Random House, 1940.

9. None But the Lonely Heart (screenplay)

a. Best Film Plays - 1945. John Gassner and Dudley

Nichols, eds. New York: Crown Publishers, 1946. 261-330.

10. Paradise Lost

a. New York: Random House, 1936.

11. Rocket to the Moon

a. New York: Dramatists Play Service, 1939.

b. New York: Random House, 1939.

12. The Silent Partner (scene)

a. New Theatre and Film 4 (Mar. 1937): 5-9.

13. Till the Day I Die

This play has not been published separately. It does

appear in various anthologies. One early anthology is:

Mayorga, Margaret Gardner, ed. Representative One-Act

Plays By American Authors. Boston: Little, Brown and Co.,

1937.

14. Waiting for Lefty

a. London: V. Gollancz, 1938. "Left Book Club Edition.

Not for sale to the public."

15. A Winter Journey

    a. London: French, 1955. (French's acting edition no. 296)

    First published in New York under the title The Country Girl (1951).

16. Six Plays of Clifford Odets

    (Includes: Waiting for Lefty, Awake and Sing!, Till the Day I Die, Paradise Lost, Golden Boy, and Rocket to the Moon)

    a. New York: The Modern Library, 1939. With Preface by Clifford Odets. "First Modern Library Edition 1939"

    b. New York: Random House, 1939.

    c. Subsequent reissues in the 1940's and 1950's of the 1939 original edition with the following half-title: "The Modern Library of the World's Best Books."

    d. New York: Grove Press, 1979.

17. Three Plays By Clifford Odets

    (Includes: Awake and Sing!, Waiting for Lefty, and Till the Day I Die)

    a. New York: Covici-Friede, 1935.

    b. New York: Random House, 1935.

18. Golden Boy, Awake and Sing!, The Big Knife

    a. Harmondsworth, Middlesex: Penguin Books, 1963.

19. "Machine Gun Reception." Rifle Rule in Cuba. With Carleton Beals.

    a. New York: Provisional Committee for Cuba, 1935.

20. Introduction. <u>Dead Souls</u>. By Nikolai Gogol.

    a. New York: The Modern Library, 1936.

21. Adaptation. <u>The Russian People</u>. By Konstantin Simonov. 1943.

    a. <u>Seven Soviet Plays</u>. Ed. Henry Wadsworth Longfellow Dana. New York: Macmillan, 1946.

22. <u>Golden Boy</u> (Musical). Adaptation by William Gibson.

    a. New York: Atheneum Press, 1965.

    b. New York: Bantam Books, 1966.

Productions of Plays

First New York productions, with number of performances in parentheses:

Waiting for Lefty. 5 Jan. 1935, Civic Repertory Theatre, New York. 26 Mar. 1935, Longacre Theatre (transferred 9 Sept. 1935 to Belasco Theatre), New York (159).

Awake and Sing!. 19 Feb. 1935, Belasco Theatre, New York (184).

Till the Day I Die. 26 Mar. 1935, Longacre Theatre, New York (135).

Paradise Lost. 9 Dec. 1935, Longacre Theatre, New York (72).

Golden Boy. 4 Nov. 1937, Belasco Theatre, New York (248).

Rocket to the Moon. 24 Nov. 1938, Belasco Theatre, New York (131).

Night Music. 22 Feb. 1940, Broadhurst Theatre, New York (20).

Clash by Night. 27 Dec. 1941, Belasco Theatre, New York (49).

The Russian People. 29 Dec. 1942, Guild Theatre, New York (39).

The Big Knife. 24 Feb. 1949, National Theatre, New York (109).

The Country Girl. 10 Nov. 1950, Lyceum Theatre, New York (235).

The Flowering Peach. 28 Dec. 1954, Belasco Theatre, New York (135).

The Silent Partner. 11 May 1972, Actors' Studio, New York (12).

Screenplays

1. The General Died at Dawn. Based on a story by Charles G. Booth. Dir. Lewis Milestone. Paramount, 1936.

2. None But the Lonely Heart. Based on a novel by Richard Llewellyn. Dir. Clifford Odets. RKO, 1944.

3. Deadline at Dawn. Based on a novel by William Irish. Dir. Harold Clurman. RKO, 1946.

4. Humoresque. Based on a story by Fannie Hurst. Zachary Gold, co-writer. Dir. Jean Negulesco. Warner Brothers, 1947.

5. The Sweet Smell of Success. Based on novelette by Ernest Lehman. Ernest Lehman, co-writer. Dir. Alexander Mackendrick. United Artists, 1957.

6. The Story on Page One. Dir. Clifford Odets. 20th Century-Fox, 1959.

7. Wild in the Country. Based on a novel by J. R. Salamanca. Dir. Philip Dunne. 20th Century-Fox, 1960.

Teleplays

1. "Big Mitch." The Richard Boone Show. NBC. 10 Dec. 1963.

2. "The Mafia Man." The Richard Boone Show. NBC. 7 Jan. 1964.

3. "The Affair. " The Richard Boone Show. NBC. Did not air.

Part Three:

Annotated Bibliography
of
Clifford Odets Scholarship

<u>Introduction</u>

This bibliography is an attempt at an exhaustive, annotated listing of any and all works relating to the life and career of Clifford Odets (1906-1963). Each category in the bibliographical essay is represented in this bibliography, with an explanation as to either its method of organization or the rationale behind its inclusion. An attempt has been made to be as objective as possible in the annotations, but sources with particular errors or biases have been duly noted. Cross-references have been kept down to a minimum, although this was unavoidable in the "Critical Studies: Individual Plays" section (reasons are given therein).

Articles by Odets

A list of articles which bear Odets' name. Beginning with this, and all subsequent sections, a "Not Examined" list can be found following the annotated entries. "Not Examined" is an accumulation of items which are known to exist but have not been scrutinized for this bibliography. In some cases, a guess has been taken as to the proper category for a particular entry.

Odets, Clifford. "All Drama Is Propaganda." Current
    Controversy 1 (Feb. 1936): 13+.
    Argues that all art, because it is made up of the
    artist's particular treatment of the theme, is a form of
    propaganda. Provides examples throughout literary
    history: ancient Greek drama, church plays, Shakespeare,
    Ibsen, etc. Comments that artists can only be
    understood by situating them in their historical time
    and place.
---. "The Awakening of the American Theatre." New Theatre

and Film: 1934-1937. Ed. Herbert Kline. New York:

Harcourt, Brace, Jovanovich, 1985. 13-15.

Odets' remarks about pre-Depression theatre which used

"art" as a commodity, and compares this to its use in

contemporary theatre. Advertises Ben Blake's The

Awakening of the American Theatre, a pamphlet about the

post-Depression theatre.

---. "'Democratic Vistas' In Drama." New York Times 21 Nov.

1937, sec. 11: 1+.

Odets praises the movie industry for its exploration of

the common man in America. He wishes that the theatre

would present a similar portrait of American life. He

insists that theatre should learn from movies.

---. "Genesis of a Play." New York Times 1 Feb. 1942, sec.

10: 3.

Odets traces the history of Clash by Night. Provides

insights into the creation of character, theme, and

plot, applying this to all of his plays. Mentions other

projects.

---. "How A Playwright Triumphs." Harper's Sept. 1966: 64-

74.

Article drawn from an interview with Arthur Wagner in

September of 1961. Odets talks about what playwriting

is all about, why he became a playwright, etc., but

refuses to talk about Hollywood. Mentions his Group

Theatre years.

---. "In Praise of a Maturing Industry." <u>New York Times</u> 6 Nov. 1955, sec. 2: 5.

Talks of the filmed version of <u>The Big Knife</u>. Odets praises Hollywood for agreeing to film this play which was originally rejected because of its attitude toward Hollywood.

---. Letter. <u>New York Times</u> 25 May 1952, sec. 2: 3.

Tribute to John Garfield in "Drama Mailbag" section. Praises Garfield's energy, character, and rise from poverty to fame (the actor had just died).

---. "On Coming Home." <u>New York Times</u> 25 July 1948, sec. 2: 1.

Odets defends his decision to go to Hollywood and to then return to New York. Talks of works in progress. Subtly knocks the superficial Hollywood life.

---. "Some Problems of the Modern Dramatist." <u>New York Times</u> 15 Dec. 1935, sec. 11: 3.

Announces his rejection of standard plot-lines and the well-made play. Notes a preference for Chekhov's style.

---. "To Whom It May Concern: Marilyn Monroe." <u>Show</u> Oct. 1962: 67+.

Requiem following Monroe's suicide. Attempts to reveal the complexity behind a seemingly "simple, movie-struck American girl" (67). Calls Monroe "homeless" (67), an attribute often associated with Odetsian protagonists (and Odets himself). Argues that Monroe was no longer a

Hollywood commodity when she began to rebel against her
stereotype.

---. "The Transient Olympian." Show Apr. 1963: 106+.
Creates a fictitious movie star, who serves as an
allegorical figure. Gives his creation Odetsian
characteristics: homelessness, alienation, spiritual
emptiness. Provides commentary on Hollywood life.

---. "Two Approaches To The Writing Of A Play." New York
Times 22 Apr. 1951, sec. 2: 1+.
Describes two impulses behind the writing of a play:
objective fabrication without personal affiliation and
the expression of a personal state of being. Provides
examples of how each impulse is applied to write a play.
Mentions the creative writing class he teaches and
expresses optimism for the American theatre based upon
his students' work.

---. "When Wolfe Came Home." New York Times 14 Sept. 1958,
sec. 2:3.
Written for the twentieth anniversary of Thomas Wolfe's
death. Odets was an honorary pall-bearer at Wolfe's
funeral. Reminisces about viewing Wolfe's body at
Wolfe's home.

Not Examined

---. "Boone, Renoir Find Common Ground." Los Angeles Times 1
Aug. 1963, sec. 4: 16.

---. "Clifford Odets Capitalizes His Whole Life." <u>New York World-Telegram</u> 19 Mar. 1935.

---. "Critics A Mystery to Clifford Odets, So He Finds Mr. Morgan and Gives Him the Works." <u>New York World-Telegram</u> 2 Mar. 1940.

---. "Willem de Kooning." <u>The Critic</u> 21 (Oct.-Nov. 1962): 37-38.

<u>See also</u> Odets, Clifford. "From the Group's Daybook." ("Politics and the Group Theatre").

Journals and Diaries

Odets, Clifford. <u>The Time Is Ripe: The 1940 Journal of</u>
    <u>Clifford Odets</u>. Ed. Walt Bode and Walt Odets. New
    York: Grove Press, 1988.
    Written by Odets with possible publication in mind, this
    is a detailing of his thoughts on everything from world
    affairs to Broadway and Hollywood. Much information on
    his process of playwriting, and the casting, rehearsing,
    and eventual New York opening of <u>Night Music</u>.
<u>See also</u> Miller, Gabriel. <u>Clifford Odets</u>. ("Critical
    Studies: General. 1964-Present").

Biographical Materials

This listing includes books and articles providing biographical information, character insights, general information, and interviews.

"Agit-Prop." Time 17 June 1935: 38.

    Chronicles the banning of Waiting for Lefty in several cities and the reaction against this by various groups around the country.

Appel, Benjamin. "Odets University." Literary Review 19 (Summer 1976): 470-75.

    Author a student in Odets' 1951 playwriting class at the Actors' Studio. Reviews Odets' teaching techniques, offers insights into his character. Includes a letter Odets wrote to Appel concerning the House Un-American Activities Committee (6/17/52).

Atkinson, Brooks. "Critic At Large." New York Times 3 Sept. 1963, sec. 1: 30.

    Argues against the notion that Odets failed on Broadway.

Maintains that he did not fail as a person. Provides some character insights and a brief discussion of Odets' hobbies. Mentions his appearance on a television show regarding the death of Marilyn Monroe, but fails to give specific details, i.e. what show? (See "Manuscripts" : "Miscellaneous Items" # 6)

Berch, Barbara. "Going Their Way Now?" New York Times 27 Aug. 1944, sec. 2: 3.

Reviews Odets' arrival in Hollywood for a one-picture deal with RKO. Notes his changing, more favorable attitude toward Hollywood. Mentions his desire to improve the caliber of motion pictures. Notes that Odets has written dozens of screenplays, but has taken credit for only a few.

Brenman-Gibson, Margaret. Clifford Odets: American Playwright: The Years from 1906 to 1940. New York: Atheneum Press, 1981.

Lengthy biographical study emphasizing the psychological factors in Odets' life. Bibliography with published and unpublished play listing and screenplay listing. Much information on the Literary Estate of Clifford Odets. Many references to psychology and history. Second volume due.

---. "Odets: Failure Or Not?" New York Times 13 June 1965, sec. 2: 1+.

Complains of the general indifference to Odets' work.

Depicts Odets as a symbolic psychological figure.

Churchill, Douglas W. "Mr. Odets Is Acclimated." New York
Times 3 May 1936, sec. 10: 4.

Odets' views on theatre and film as media; film is more
advanced, he believes. Notes upcoming projects.
Rejects the argument that he was lured to Hollywood by
the money.

"Clifford Odets." Wilson Bulletin 11 (1937): 374.

Brief biographical sketch. Mentions Chekhov influence
and Odets' reaction to it. Odets' hobbies are
discussed.

"Clifford Odets, Playwright, Dies." New York Times 16 Aug.
1963, sec. 1: 27.

Odets' obituary. Standard life details. Notes that
Odets, in 30 years, never outgrew the term "promising."
His "ghost writing" is discussed.

Clurman, Harold. All People Are Famous. New York: Harcourt,
Brace, Jovanovich, 1974.

Clurman's autobiography. Biographical details of Odets'
home life, hobbies, character quirks, etc. Talks of
HUAC testimony and Odets' political convictions.

---. "Clifford Odets." New York Times 25 Aug. 1963, sec. 2:
1.

Clurman's eulogy for Odets. Describes him as a highly
personal playwright.

---. "Clifford Odets." Saturday Review 14 Sept. 1963: 10.

Brief remembrances of Odets as a friend and colleague.

"Credo of a Wrong-Living Man." _Time_ 14 Dec. 1962: 40.

Announcement of Odets' signing with NBC as a script
supervisor of a new Richard Boone television show.
Odets offers his views on present-day theatre and how to
improve it.

"'55 Pulitzer Jury Chose Odets Play." _New York Times_ 18 Aug.
1963, sec. 1: 80.

Reports that the 1955 Pulitzer Prize jury voted _The
Flowering Peach_ as the award winner, but was overruled
by the Pulitzer Advisory Board. Cover-up noted; Odets
never knew that this took place.

Gibson, William. "A Memento." Preface. _Golden Boy: The
Book of a Musical_. By Gibson and Clifford Odets. New
York: Atheneum Press, 1965.

Chronicles the problems of adapting a straight play into
a musical. Indicates that Odets was planning the _Golden
Boy_ musical as a return to the stage. Recounts his
taking over of libretto after Odets' death. Fond
remembrances, some character insights.

Gould, Jean. _Modern American Playwrights_. New York: Dodd,
Mead and Co., 1966. 186-187.

Chapter 9 devoted to Clifford Odets. Brief biographical
sketch and career highlights. Contains some errors.

Hewes, Henry. "American Playwrights Self-Appraised."
Saturday Review 3 Sept. 1955: 18-19.

Odets, along with 18 other American playwrights, answers
questionnaire concerning theatre: advice to new
playwrights, steps for better playwriting, favorite
play, favorite playwright, current trends in
playwriting.

Kauffmann, Stanley. "Is Artistic Integrity Enough?" New
Republic 8 Feb. 1960: 22.

Movie review of The Story on Page One (Odets wrote and
directed). Notes that the theatre misses Odets
desperately.

Mantle, Burns. Contemporary American Playwrights. New York:
Dodd, Mead and Co., 1939. 115-121.

Provides biographical material on Odets as an actor and
fledgling playwright. Notes that Odets is "the most
promising talent" to come into theatre in a decade
(115), and cites Odets' exclusive theatre background as
a major reason. Provides production dates and
information for all plays up until Golden Boy.

McCarten, John. "Revolution's Number One Boy." New Yorker
22 Jan. 1938: 21+.

Odets voices his discontent with the contemporary
theatre. Describes early novel, later destroyed, which
was reworked into Golden Boy. Some background
information on Odets' family life. Odetsian character
quirks highlighted.

Mendelsohn, Michael J. "Odets At Center Stage: A Talk With

Michael J. Mendelsohn." <u>Theatre Arts</u> May 1963: 16+,
June 1963: 28+.

Interview with Odets for Mendelsohn's dissertation (<u>see</u>
<u>also</u> "Dissertations"). Odets offers views on writing,
directing, contemporary theatre, George Jean Nathan (a
very hostile attitude), the adapting of a play (<u>The</u>
<u>Russian People</u>), the influence of Victor Hugo, the
Bible, Hollywood, television, the missing scene in the
published version of <u>Waiting for Lefty</u>, etc. Much
information; beware of the Odets tendency to fantasize
and forget.

---. "Odets: The Artist in Wonderland." <u>Drama Critique</u> 9
(Winter 1966): 31-34.

Discussion of Odets' final move to Hollywood in 1955,
the reasons behind this decision to go, and the total
output of his Hollywood years from 1936-1961 (he may
have worked on dozens of films). Brief review of films
<u>None But the Lonely Heart</u>, <u>Humoresque</u>, and <u>The Story on</u>
<u>Page One</u>.

Miller, Arthur. <u>Timebends: A Life</u>. New York: Grove Press,
1987.

Describes personal encounters with Odets: one in which
Odets claims to be working on a play about Woodrow
Wilson, and one where Odets was a featured speaker at a
1949 peace conference. Compares Odets with O'Neill in
terms of style, temperament, and degree of social

commitment. Praises Odets' poetry and his unique use of
language. Some information about the Group Theatre is
offered.

"Odets, Indignant, Plans New Inquiry." New York Times 7 July
1935, sec. 2: 2.

Odets denounces American Ambassadors in Cuba. Accuses
the United States of collusion with the Mendieta regime.
Tells of plans to organize another delegation to Cuba
and to write a play about the Cuban situation.

Peary, Gerald. "Odets Of Hollywood." Sight and Sound 56
(Winter 1986/87): 59-63.

Discusses the reasons behind Odets' move to Hollywood
and outlines his career there. Notes Odets' work on
various scripts at various studios, including many
uncredited writings. Some commentary on all produced
Odets scripts, especially The General Died at Dawn and
None But the Lonely Heart. Describes the move to
Hollywood as a sell-out and a waste of time and talent.

Peck, Ira. "'The Theatre Did Not Want Clifford Odets.'" New
York Times 18 Oct. 1964, sec. 2: 1.

Title is quote from William Gibson, who offers
personalized remembrances and an evaluation of Odets as
a playwright. Gibson complains that the theatre did not
support Odets, forcing him to go to Hollywood. Notes
Odets' struggle between art and materialism. Gibson
relates problems in changing Golden Boy from Italian to

Black and from straight play to musical.

Perkoff, Leslie. "I Would Like To Tell The Truth: Interview With Clifford Odets." World Film News 3 (Aug. 1938): 146-147.

Odets offers his observations on film as a medium and the films he would like to make. Discussion of England's response to Odets' plays and films, most notably The General Died at Dawn.

"Pirandello Avoids Debate On Politics." New York Times 24 July 1935, sec. 1: 20.

Odets, along with a group of left-wing American playwrights, debate Italian playwright, Luigi Pirandello, on the topic of art and artists. Pirandello refuses to talk about fascism and war or to mix art and politics. He does, however, praise Odets' plays, "not because they are social, but because they are artistic."

Schumach, Murray. "Hollywood Gets Unusual Praise." New York Times 1 Oct. 1959, sec. 1: 39.

Odets, working on The Story on Page One, speaks highly of the movie industry. Notes that Odets has authored about 15 movie scripts.

Semple, Lorenzo, Jr. "After 15 Years." Theatre Arts Monthly 34 (Dec. 1950): 30-31.

Odets, rehearsing The Country Girl, discusses his technique of playwriting and reveals the titles of his next three plays ("They even have titles which won't be

changed" [31]): <u>By the Sea</u>, <u>The Seasons</u>, and <u>The Tides</u>
<u>of Fundy</u>. Author notes a mellowing in Odets' character
from his Group Theatre days, commenting that he is less
idealistic and more of a "practical theatre man" (30).

Shuman, R[obert] Baird. "Clifford Odets: From Influence to
Affluence." <u>Modern American Drama: Essays In Criticism</u>.
Ed. William E. Taylor. Florida: Everett/Edwards, Inc.,
1968. 39-46.

Focuses on Odets' dependency on the Group Theatre and
vice versa, and his tendency to write allegory. Remarks
that Odets will be long remembered. Provides
biographical material about Odets in the early 1930's.

Sugrue, Thomas. "Mr. Odets Regrets: A Social Drama in One
Act." <u>American Magazine</u> 122 (Oct. 1936): 42+.
Interview written in play form. Odets provides
biographical details and talks about his early attempts
at poetry and novel writing. Discusses his jobs in
radio and theatre and offers a brief history of the
Group Theatre. He sidesteps the question, "Are you a
Communist?" His failure to stick to one subject is
handled comically.

"Three New Yorks." <u>New York Times</u> 31 Mar. 1940, mag sec: 6+.
Odets, Elmer Rice, and William Saroyan answer the
question of what makes New York so distinctive. Odets
describes New York in musical terms. Some observations
on Odets' writing habits.

"White Hope." Time 5 Dec. 1938: 44+.

>   Odets on cover; caption: "Clifford Odets--Down With The
>   General Fraud!" Notes that in the three years since
>   Lefty, Odets is still the most promising playwright in
>   America. Praise of Odets' dialogue. Odets' offers
>   opinions on contemporary theatre and vows not to return
>   to Hollywood.

See also Weales, Gerald. Clifford Odets: Playwright.

>   ("Critical Studies: General. 1964-Present").

Not Examined

Beebe, Lucius. "The Prolific Mr. O." New York Herald
>   Tribune 31 Mar. 1935.

Farrell, James T. "More About Clifford Odets." New Theatre
>   June 1935.

Lerner, Max. "My Friend Clifford Odets." San Francisco
>   Examiner 29 Aug. 1963.

Usigli, Rodolfo. "Mis encuentros con Clifford Odets."
>   Hispania 46 (1963): 689-92.

Critical Studies: General

An overview of themes, motifs, and influences as noted in full-length studies and/or scholarly articles. These works are basically reviews of the entire Odets canon. Many contain valuable information about individual plays, as well. This section is divided into the following categories: "1935-1940," "1941-1950," "1951-1963," "1964-Present," and the reasons for doing so are related in the bibliographical essay.

1935-1940

Atkinson, Brooks. New York Times 26 Mar. 1939, sec. 10: 1.
    Argues that Odets is a writer who is not dependent on plot and story. Discusses the quality of improvisation in his writing. Notes the Group Theatre's standing in the world of theatre and how much it owes its success to Odets.

Block, Anita. The Changing World in Plays and Theatre.
    Boston: Little, Brown and Co., 1939.

Praises Odets as the playwright who will challenge
Eugene O'Neill, showing certain similarities between the
two playwrights. Labels Odets a social dramatist with a
dynamic quality and a gift for dialogue.

Brown, John Mason. Two On The Aisle. New York: W. W. Norton
and Co., 1938.

Notes that Odets' talent is equaled only by his
resentment of "The System" (197). Mentions his
Chekhovian style and describes him as a powerful,
attention-getting dramatist. Comments reprinted in
Dramatis Personae (1963).

Ferguson, Otis. "Pay-Off On Odets." New Republic 27 Sept.
1939: 216-17, 4 Oct. 1939: 242-3.

Book review of Six Plays Of Clifford Odets. High praise
for Odets; he "holds the corner on the genius of serious
writing for the theatre today" (243).

Gassner, John. "The American Galaxy." Masters Of The Drama.
New York: Dover Publications, 1940. 662-699.

Describes Odets as "the foremost discovery of the
thirties" (689). Notes that Odets is driven by an
"angry vision," which is both a strength and a flaw
(691). Presents the positive and negative aspects of
his dialogue. Notes a mellowing trend from Lefty to
Rocket.

Isaacs, Edith J. R. "Clifford Odets: First Chapters."
Theatre Arts Monthly 23 (April 1939): 257-264.

Study which determines Odets' faults as a playwright as well as his creative qualities. Among his faults: no accurate picture of the middle-class; little character development. Creative qualities include: vibrant, theatrical speech; intention to create purposeful drama. Provides a brief character study for every play until Rocket.

Krutch, Joseph Wood. The American Drama Since 1918. New York: Random House, 1939.

Krutch believes that Odets will get better and better as a dramatist. Notes a move away from Marxism toward more "traditional virtues of the drama" (315).

---. "The Theatre." America Now. Ed. Harold E. Stearns. New York: Charles Scribner's Sons, 1938. 72-81.

Comments that Odets is the most promising playwright in America who possesses an actor's instinct for the purely theatrical. Suggests a Chekhovian influence. Argues that he is the best of the revolutionary playwrights, not because of his politics, but because he is the best writer.

Lawson, John H. Theory and Technique of Playwriting. 1936. New York: Hill and Wang, 1960.

Comments that Odets is more of a scenewright than a playwright. Notes a progression problem in the plays, citing this as a general problem of modern playwrights. Describes Odets as brilliant for "heightening the effect of a scene by underscoring the emotional strain" (227).

Mersand, Joseph. Tradition in American Literature. 1939.
New York: Kennikat Press, Inc., 1968.
Notes that critics, while heaping praise upon Odets, have failed to determine the extent of his contribution to American drama. Highlights Odets' strengths as a dramatist: ideas, dialogue, social significance.

Nathan, George Jean. Encyclopaedia Of The Theatre. New York: Alfred A. Knopf, 1940.
Claims that Odets, while talented, was no genius and could not live up to all that was expected of him.

---. "The White Hope Gets Paler." Newsweek 4 Mar. 1940: 42.
Begins as a review of Night Music, but becomes an overview of Odets' career up to that point. Echoes sentiments of Encyclopaedia Of The Theatre: Odets fails to live up to his own reputation.

Vernon, Grenville. "The Case of Clifford Odets." Commonweal 28 (10 June 1938): 188.
Notes Odets' faith in himself as the "White Hope of the American Theatre." Comments that Odets should stop blowing his own horn and should return from Hollywood in spirit. Notices a decline since Awake and Sing!.

---. "Clifford Odets." Commonweal 29 (16 Dec. 1938): 215.
Notes that little has been written about the fact that Odets' plays are Jewish. Argues that he will not write the great American play because he cannot distance

himself from his Jewish characters; his "American" or "Italian" creations are Jewish in thought or expression.

Young, Stark. "New Talents." New Republic 29 May 1935: 78.

Talks of the critical reception of Odets' work since the publication of the Covici-Friede edition of Three Plays By Clifford Odets. Notes how amusing it would be if he were the only critic to see redeeming values in Odets' work. Claims that "Odets is one of the few American playwrights who is worth thinking about at all."

Not Examined

Fadiman, Clifton. "The Problem Play From Ibsen to Odets." Stage Feb. 1936.

1941-1950

Gassner, John. "The Long Journey of a Talent." Theatre Arts Monthly July 1949: 25+.

Focuses on the allegory in Odets' plays, noting that too much allegorizing flaws his work. Comments that he must stop looking toward the horizon in order to write meaningful plays. Notes a discrepancy between presented facts and Odets' interpretation of them, which tends to be a problem in the plays. Good studies of individual plays.

Meister, Charles W. "Comparative Drama: Chekhov, Shaw, Odets." Poet Lore 55 (1950): 249-257.

Argues that Odets relies on Chekhovian techniques such as disconnected dialogue and the creation of dramatic atmosphere as the basis for his plays. Comments that Awake and Sing! incorporates these techniques better than Paradise Lost, which is usually considered Odets' Chekhovian play. Argues that Odets' understanding is shallower than Chekhov's.

Mersand, Joseph. The American Drama Since 1930. 1949. New York: Kennikat Press, Inc., 1968.

Extremely high praise for Odets. Calls for further study, evaluation, and classification of Odets' work. Notes that critics placed too much hope on Odets while he was too young to achieve it. Mentions Chekhov influence.

Morris, Lloyd. Postscript to Yesterday. America: The Last Fifty Years. New York: Random House, 1947. 172-213.

Comments that both conservatives and Communists found little to praise in Odets' plays. Argues that his vision was abstract; he expressed "a poetic intuition rather than a political formula" (201). Some form of collective action seen as the only solution offered to the problems presented in the plays. Notes that there is nothing new about Odets' vision or prophecy except his method of presentation.

Slochower, Harry. No Voice Is Wholly Lost. London: Dennis Dobson, Ltd., 1946.

A study of Odets' characters. Notes that while they are
not wanted, Odets' characters never lose faith in
themselves or their fellow man and all experience a
rebirth in some way.

Warshow, Robert S. "Poet of the Jewish Middle Class."

Commentary May 1946: 17-22.

Views Odets' importance in terms of American Jewish
literature. Notes that Odets presents three-dimensional
Jewish characters -- something rare outside of Yiddish
theatre.

1951-1963

Agee, James. Agee On Film. New York: McDowell, Obolensky,
1958.

Brief reviews of None But the Lonely Heart (128) and
Deadline at Dawn (197), originally written for The
Nation. Calls None an "almost-perfect film" and praises
Odets' love for the characters in his film. Finds fault
with his excesses of sentimentality. Odets' writing in
Deadline at Dawn is described as "pure ham," but the
movie is termed "likable."

Brown, John Mason. Dramatis Personae. New York: The Viking
Press, 1963.

Comments from Two On The Aisle (1938) reprinted.

Brustein, Robert. "America's New Culture Hero." Commentary
Feb. 1958: 123+.

Describes the new American protagonist: an inarticulate
hero, born in an underprivileged environment, who has
lost political and vocal power. Notes that Odets'
protagonists, because of their verbosity and interest in
political and social causes, do not embody this new type
of hero.

Clurman, Harold. The Naked Image. New York: MacMillan Co.,
1958.

Characterizes all of Odets' work as a "self-portrayal"
(271). Describes the essence of his work as moral, not
political. Disputes the Chekhov connection.

Hughes, Catharine. "Odets: The Price of Success."
Commonweal 78 (20 Sept. 1963): 558-560.

Notes that Odets failed to outgrow the term "promising"
and the notion that he "sold out" to Hollywood.
Describes him as a typical American writer--one who ages
but does not mature. Mentions that the later works were
unfairly judged against the earlier successes.

Hunt, Albert. "Only Soft-Centered Left." Encore 8 (May-June
1961): 5-12.

Discusses the reasons why Odets' plays have dated so
badly. Notes an ultimate lack of social commitment on
Odets' part and a limited artistic talent which created
superficial characters and preconceived generalizations
about society. Comments that Odets was seeking a wider
audience which led to his decision to go to Hollywood.

McCarthy, Mary. <u>Sights and Spectacles 1937-1958</u>. London: W.

    H. Heinemann Ltd., 1959.

    Extremely critical of Odets' abilities. Claims that

    Odets never could leave the framework of what he knew

    (the Bronx, Jews). Argues that every play is simply a

    reworking of <u>Awake and Sing!</u>. Comments reprinted in

    <u>Mary McCarthy's Theatre Chronicles: 1937-1962</u>. New

    York: Farrar, Straus and Co., 1963.

Mendelsohn, Michael J. "Clifford Odets and the American

    Family." <u>Drama Survey</u> 3 (Fall 1963): 238-243.

    Argues that Odets used the family as his "principal

    medium for expression" (239). Notes Odets' shift "away

    from anti-family rebellion and toward pro-family

    solidarity" during the 1940's (242).

Nathan, George Jean. <u>The Theatre in the Fifties</u>. New York:

    Alfred A. Knopf: 1953. 55-57.

    Notes Odets' talent, but comments that he writes "purely

    commercial drama" (53). Faults him for having a limited

    imagination and a flair for melodrama. Predicts that he

    will be wholly forgotten in due time.

Shuman, R[obert] Baird. <u>Clifford Odets</u>. New York: Twayne

    Publishers, Inc., 1962.

    The first full-length study devoted entirely to Odets.

    Stresses the family element in all of his dramas. Some

    biographical data. Brief, annotated bibliography.

    According to Gerald Weales, this source is "shockingly

full of factual errors" (<u>Playwright</u> 197).   Some
misleading annotations.

Sievers, W. David.   <u>Freud On Broadway</u>.   New York: Hermitage
House, 1955.

Subjects Odets' work to Freudian analysis.   Discovers
Odets' "indebtedness to Freud's psychological world-
view" (17).   Notes Odets' progression away from
propaganda and towards insights of psychology.   Good
psychological analysis of many individual plays.

Weales, Gerald.   <u>American Drama Since World War Two</u>.   New
York: Harcourt, Brace and World, Inc., 1962.

Argues that none of Odets' postwar work displays the
optimism of the plays of the 1930's.   Describes Lorraine
Hansberry's <u>A Raisin In The Sun</u> as a latter-day Odets
drama.

<u>Not Examined</u>

Chiesa Lasorsa, Paola.   "Il Teatro di Clifford Odets."   <u>Studi
Americani</u> 7 (1961): 363-409.

<u>1964-Present</u>

Bigsby, C. W. E.   <u>A Critical Introduction to Twentieth-
Century American Drama</u>.   2 vols.   Cambridge: Cambridge
University Press, 1982.

Notes the dilemma between Odets the realist and Odets
the visionary.   Describes his ambiguity--visions lack

sharpness, dreams lack power. Compares Odets to Elmer Rice.

Bigsby, Christopher. "The Collapse of Ideals. Christopher Bigsby Discusses the Current Popularity of Clifford Odets." <u>Times Higher Education Supplement</u> (London) 11 May 1984: 16.

Notes sudden popularity in London of American plays from the 1930's and 1940's and discusses their significance to a contemporary audience. Argues that Odets' characters compare favorably to those of O'Neill, Miller, and Williams in that they sense their alienation in a complex society. Hints that Odets was never a true radical and wanted a morally better world "in Roosevelt's sense rather than Marx's."

Cantor, Harold. <u>Clifford Odets: Playwright-Poet</u>. New Jersey: Scarecrow Press, 1978.

Full-length study which forgoes the traditional play-by-play analysis. Focuses on themes and motifs found in the entire Odets canon. Extensive bibliography.

---. "Odets' Yinglish: The Psychology of Dialect as Dialogue." <u>Studies in American Jewish Literature</u> 2 (1982): 61-68.

Comments that Odets created a living, memorable dialogue through Yiddish-English. He used then-unknown verb variations, inverted sentence order, and prepositional changes and omissions in order to create both comic relief and a new "art-language from Yiddish roots" (63).

Cohn, Ruby. Dialogue In American Drama. Bloomington:

Indiana University Press, 1971.

Generally dismisses Odets' use of language as not

deserving of extensive analysis. However, notes the

Jewish-American syntax and vocabulary of Odets' early

works. Argues that with success, Odets lost his ear for

this idiom. Names Arthur Miller as Odets' successor in

terms of Jewish dialogue.

Curley, Dorothy Nyren, et al., eds. A Library of Literary

Criticism: Modern American Literature. 4th ed. 3 vols.

New York: Frederick Ungar Publishing Co., 1969. 2: 437-

444.

A selection of reviews from various points in Odets'

career providing a brief overview of the critical

response to his work. Researchers should beware that an

error occurs: The Country Wife should read The Country

Girl.

Freedman, Morris. American Drama in Social Context.

Carbondale: Southern Illinois University Press, 1971.

Argues that Odets never achieved a universality in his

plays. Depicts him as a forerunner of Miller and

Williams. Notes that only stray speeches will remain of

Odets' legacy.

Goldstein, Malcolm. "Body and Soul on Broadway." Modern

Drama 7 (Feb. 1965): 411-21.

Argues that Odets, like most other social protest
writers of the 1930's, contributed little to economic
and social philosophy; Odets' contribution was to
"theatrical artistry" (421). Claims that in his early
plays, Odets passed over psychological problems to
pursue social questions. Moving with the demands of
theatre conventions, Odets began to give "equal weight
to social and psychological problems" (414).

---. "The Playwrights of the 1930's." The American Theater
Today. Ed. Alan S. Downer. New York: Basic Books,
Inc., 1967.
Faults Odets' solutions to problems as being vague and
lacking of an appropriate plan. Notes the dated quality
of his work.

Griffin, Robert J. "On The Love Songs of Clifford Odets."
The Thirties: Fiction, Poetry, Drama. Ed. Warren
French. Deland, Florida: Everett Edwards, Inc., 1967.
Notes that "Odets became an imaginative spokesman ... of
the romance of the '30s ..." (199). Remarks that
Hollywood was Odets' downfall. Compares him to O'Casey
rather than Chekhov.

Kazin, Alfred. Starting Out in the Thirties. New York:
Atlantic-Little, Brown: 1965. 80-82.
High praise for Odets' ability to excite an audience
through lively stage presentations. Discusses audience
response to Awake and Lefty.

Lewis, Allan. American Plays and Playwrights of the
    Contemporary Theatre. New York: Crown Publishing,
    1970.
    Remarks that Odets, after Hollywood period, was no
    longer as influential as he had once been. Comments
    that he was too weak to become a great playwright;
    "Odets betrayed his own talent" (113).

Lumley, Frederick. New Trends in Twentieth Century Drama.
    3rd ed. New York: Oxford University Press, 1969.
    Argues that in all Odets' plays actions are governed by
    economic circumstances. Notes Odets' biases, but
    remarks that he did not substitute propaganda for good
    theatre.

Maloff, Saul. "Stormbird of the Working Class." Commonweal
    3 Dec. 1971: 226-229.
    Complains of major, personal disappointment after Odets
    cooperated at the HUAC hearing. Labels Odets a Messiah
    of sorts in the 1930's, who later could not satisfy even
    his most loyal followers (like the author). Describes
    him as "the American Chekhov" (226). Favorable review
    of Gerald Weales' Clifford Odets: Playwright.

---. "The Thirties and Clifford Who?" Commonweal 8 Oct.
    1982: 531-535.
    As title indicates, argues that Odets is all but
    forgotten today. Labels him an "erratically gifted
    minor writer" (532). Describes his cooperation with the

HUAC as "moral collapse" (532). Reviews Brenman-
Gibson's <u>Clifford Odets: American Playwright</u>. Finds it
"dismayingly unsatisfying" due to its overuse of
psychological jargon and explanations (533).

Mendelsohn, Michael J. "Clifford Odets: The Artist's
Commitment." <u>Literature and Society</u>. Ed. Bernice
Slote. Lincoln: University of Nebraska Press, 1964.
Portrays Odets' work as a mixture of "proletarianism,
humanitarianism, and intellectualism" (142). Focuses on
Odets' optimism and faith in the common man. Examines
his commitment to "the lost and fallen in American
society" (144).

---. <u>Clifford Odets: Humane Dramatist</u>. Florida: Everett-
Edwards, 1969.
Stresses the humaneness, not the radicalism of Odets'
work. Commentary is accentuated by passages from
interview with Odets (<u>see also</u> "Odets At Center Stage"
in "Biographical Materials"). Discusses Odets'
influence on American drama and Chekhov's influence on
Odets. Provides information on his Hollywood and
television careers.

Miller, Gabriel. <u>Clifford Odets</u>. New York: Continuum
Publishing Co., 1989.
Acknowledges the critical rejection of Odets' work and
attempts to counter this by presenting Odets as a
playwright who experimented with dramatic form and with

various genres. Devotes entire chapters to the Chekhov
influence and to the 1940 journal (see also "Journals
and Diaries"). References made to unpublished works,
screenplays, and teleplays.

Murray, Edward. Clifford Odets: The Thirties and After.
New York: Frederick Ungar, 1968.
Focuses on certain themes in Odets' dramas: men failing
to be wholly masculine, loneliness, hope for mankind.
Refutes the notion that Odets' characters are
autobiographical. Notes maturing by the time of The
Flowering Peach. Argues that Odets gave expression to a
vision of twentieth century life.

Pradhan, N[arindar] S. Modern American Drama: A Study in
Myth and Tradition. New Delhi: Arnold Hein, 1978.
Argues that Odets views the loss of an American paradise
in terms which are charged with nostalgia and proposes
revolutionary means in order to regain that paradise.
Notes his awareness of a bad economic system and how it
has brought about the disintegration of the human
personality. Comments that in his later plays, economic
loss is no longer the central theme; it is replaced by a
more moral vision about the dispossession of man's
character, tempered with a hope for a better tomorrow.
Notes a parallel with Arthur Miller and comments on
Odets' fascination with Biblical materials.

Shuman, R[obert] Baird. "Clifford Odets and the Jewish

Context." <u>From Hester Street to Hollywood</u>. Ed. Sarah

Blecher Cohen. Bloomington: Indiana University Press,

1983. 85-105.

Reviews Odets' Jewish background and use of a dialect

that he heard at home. Discusses prominent themes in

Jewish culture as they apply to Odets' work. Argues

that he lost his Jewish identity in Hollywood. Notes

that thanks to Odets, Jews were presented as human

beings rather than caricatures.

---. "Clifford Odets: A Playwright and His Jewish

Background." <u>South Atlantic Quarterly</u> 71 (Spring 1972):

225-33.

Argues that Odets' plays became less Jewish after <u>Awake</u>

<u>and Sing!</u> until <u>The Flowering Peach</u>, which returned to

Jewish themes. Describes major themes of the Jewish

background: alienation, homelessness, etc., and applies

these to his plays. Discusses his Jewish upbringing.

---. "Thematic Consistency in Odets' Early Plays." <u>Revue des</u>

<u>Langues Vivantes</u> 35 (1969): 415-20.

Discusses the major themes of Odets' earliest plays

(<u>Lefty</u>, <u>Awake</u>, <u>Paradise</u>, and <u>Till Day I Die</u>):

isolation, loneliness, and man's struggle for personal

fulfillment.

Weales, Gerald. <u>Clifford Odets: Playwright</u>. New York:

Pegasus, 1971. Rpt. <u>Odets: The Playwright</u>. New York:

Methuen Press, 1985.

Stresses homelessness and alienation theme in Odets'
work. Mentions Odets' optimism and hope for mankind.
Provides much biographical information. Discounts
usefulness of previous full-length studies (Shuman,
Mendelsohn, and Murray). Reviewed by Saul Maloff in
"Stormbird of the Working Class" (1971).

Willet, Ralph. "Clifford Odets and Popular Culture." South
Atlantic Quarterly 69 (Winter 1970): 68-78.
Demonstrates Odets' use of Hollywood and comic strip
references in plays. Shows that images of popular
culture counterpoint the despair and insecurity of the
characters. Argues that Odets tried to demonstrate how
mass culture creates hopes that capitalism denies.
Notes that while Hollywood provided new forms, themes,
and environments for his characters, Odets "succumbed to
total despair" by the end of his Hollywood career (77).

Not Examined

Goldstone, Richard H. "The Making of Americans: Clifford
Odets' Implicit Theme." Proceedings of the IVth
Congress of the International Comparative Literature
Association, 1966.

Potter, Vilma. "Baldwin and Odets: The High Cost of
'Crossing.'" California English Journal 1 (1965): 37-
41.

Reggiani, Renee, and Luciantonio Ruggieri. "Clifford Odets

tra New Deal e Nazismo." <u>Teatro della resistenza e</u>

   <u>della guerriglia</u>. Venice: Marsilio, 1977.

Sato, Susumu. "The 'Awakening' Theme in Clifford Odets and

   Arthur Miller." <u>American Literature in the 1940s</u>.

   Annual Report. Tokyo: Tokyo Chapter, American

   Literature Society of Japan, 1975.

Vogel, Arthur. "Clifford Odets: The Tragic Dilemma."

   <u>Jewish Currents</u> Jan. 1964.

Critical Studies: Individual Plays

An alphabetical listing with year of first production in parentheses. The following sources are basically studies which focus on no more than three plays. Further information may be found in any of the full-length studies annotated in "Critical Studies: General" (Cantor, Mendelsohn, Murray, Shuman).

Performance reviews are limited to opening night reviews in most major New York newspapers. Post-1940 reviews taken from New York Theatre Critics Reviews do not include page numbers, as none are offered in that publication. Reviews of revivals are not included unless some new light is shed on a particular play as a result of the revival. Additonal sources for opening night and revival reviews can be found in: Salem, James M. A Guide to Critical Reviews. 2nd ed. New Jersey: Scarecrow Press, 1973.

A number of entries, as stated before, include critiques of more than one play. For these entries, cross-references are provided. The cross-referenced entries are annotated once, under the heading of the play which it focuses on, or which it mentions first. The annotation will include information about all plays mentioned in that entry.

Awake and Sing! (1935)

Atkinson, Brooks. Rev. of Awake and Sing!. Belasco Theatre, New York. New York Times 20 Feb. 1935: 23.

Notes Odets' ability as a dramatist and an "uncommon strength in [his] dialogue." However, comments that the play lacks clarity, simplicity, and fluidity, and is "deficient in plain, theatre emotion."

---. New York Times 10 Mar. 1935, sec. 8: 1.

Comments that while his play is "not completely fulfilled nor thoroughly expressed," Odets is still the most promising playwright in America because of the strength of his character portraits. Expresses a bewilderment about the motive and logic of the play and questions its effectiveness as revolutionary drama. Compares Awake with Lefty and finds it to be the "bigger of the two" because it has less to do with political ideology and more to do with "the common humanities of life."

---. Rev. of Awake and Sing!. Windsor Theatre, New York. New York Times 8 Mar. 1939: 18.

Discussion of play's revival by the Group Theatre. Argues that with the exception of, perhaps, Golden Boy and the first act of Rocket, Odets has written nothing better than Awake.

Burt, David J. "Odets' Awake and Sing!" Explicator 27 (1968): Item 29.

Argues that ending of Awake not "tacked on," but prepared for through the use of dramatic diction and dialogue.

Clurman, Harold. "Three Introductions." Six Plays of Clifford Odets. New York: The Modern Library, 1939.

Argues that Awake is not a depressing play, and is rather true to life. Disputes Chekhov comparison claiming that the plays of Sean O'Casey make for a better comparison with Odets' work. Defines "middle-class" as depicted in Paradise. Element of love prevents play from becoming too depressing. Calls its ending positive, although weak. Notes allegory in Golden Boy. Examines opinions of that play, and tests their validity.

Cohn, Ruby and Bernard F. Dukore. Twentieth Century Drama: England, Ireland, and the United States. New York: Random House, 1966. 219-274.

Brief discussion of Odets' career with the Group Theatre and his move to Hollywood. Notes agit-prop motif and use of family in Awake, which follows essay, pp. 224-274. Credits Odets a pioneer in the use of a dramatic

dialogue which successfully captures the rhythms of
urban speech.

Davidson, Clifford, et al., eds. <u>Drama in the Twentieth
Century</u>. New York: AMS Press, 1984.

Brief argument for <u>Awake</u> as poetry.

Drew, Elizabeth. <u>Discovering Drama</u>. New York: W. W. Norton,
1937.

Brief consideration of Odets, especially in relation to
Chekhov. Only <u>Awake</u> and <u>Lefty</u> are discussed.

Downer, Alan, S. <u>Fifty Years of American Drama: 1900-1950</u>.
Chicago: Henry Regnery Co., 1951.

Calls <u>Awake</u> "an astonishing achievement for a first
play" (62). Virtually ignores Odets over the 50-year
period.

Dozier, Richard J. "The Making of <u>Awake and Sing!</u>." <u>The
Markham Review</u> 6 (1977): 61-65.

Analyzes the major changes that <u>I Got The Blues</u>
underwent to become <u>Awake and Sing!</u>. Argues that <u>Awake</u>
is a richer, more unified, and more complex version.

Farmer, Mary Virginia. Rev. of <u>Awake and Sing!</u>. <u>New Theatre</u>
3 (March 1935): 20.

Praises the play, but describes some technical problems
inherent in it that were noticeable in its first
production. Predicts that Odets' next play will make
him "the leading revolutionary playwright in America."

Freedman, Morris. <u>The Moral Impulse</u>. Carbondale and

Edwardsville: Southern Illinois University Press, 1967.
Argues that familial situations and overbearing mother
figure obscure the theme of Awake. Details certain
ambiguous elements in the play.

Gassner, John. The Theatre In Our Times. New York: Crown
Publishers, Inc., 1954.
Notes that Odets strives for, and achieves, universality
in Awake. Discusses "tag-ending" of play. Reviews 1951
re-staging of Golden Boy. Reprints comments from "The
Long Journey of a Talent" (see also "Critical Studies:
General"-"1941-1950").

Gross, Theodore L., ed. The Literature of American Jews.
New York: The Free Press, 1973. 113-167.
Brief discussion of Odets' career with some biographical
details. The complete text of Awake follows: 115-167.
Comments that Awake is concerned with the Jewish
immigrant experience and that the play rises above the
heading "proletarian drama."

Haslam, Gerald W. "Odets' Use of Yiddish-English in Awake
and Sing!" Research Studies of Washington State
University 34 (Sept. 1966): 161-164.
Notes that "Odets produced an acceptable stage version
of Yiddish-English that caught the poetry, as well as
the structure, of the actual dialect" (161). Defines
"Yiddish-English" as an essentially American English

language with Yiddish grammar and lexicons, and describes the structure of this language.

Kaplan, Charles. "Two Depression Plays and Broadway's Popular Idealism." American Quarterly 15 (Winter 1963): 579-85.

Demonstrates how Awake is representative of its time. Compares Awake with You Can't Take It With You.

Krutch, Joseph Wood. "Awake and Sing!" Nation 140 (Mar. 13, 1935): 314-16.

Describes Awake as the characteristic play of the 1930's generation of revolutionary plays.

Lee, Vera. "Boretz and Murray and Odets in Boston." Drama Critique 11 (Winter 1968): 40-43.

Brief interview with Michael Murray who directed a revival of Awake at the Charles St. Theatre in Boston. Murray argues that the play speaks to the young people of the '60's almost as directly as it did to the youth of the 1930's.

O'Hara, Frank H. Today in American Drama. Chicago: University of Chicago Press, 1939. 53-141.

Analysis of Awake as a comedy. Notes that it is not an uplifting, "happy ending" comedy, but rather a sobering play. Praises its structure which allows propaganda to enter subtly.

"Odets Play In London." New York Times 21 Feb. 1938: 15.

Argues that the play protests too much and that this

production suffered from the mixed English-American cast.

Pearce, Richard. "Pylon, Awake and Sing!, and the Apocalyptic Imagination of the '30s." Criticism 13 (Spring 1971): 131-41.

Describes Awake as a work which develops the feeling of apocalypse, so common in the literature of the 1930's. Cites Odets' brilliance in dramatizing two forces (outside and inside) at work in the play.

Scanlan, Tom. Family, Drama, and American Dreams. Connecticut: Greenwood Press, 1978. 184-189.

Discusses the family life depicted in Awake and the way Odets used the institution of family to express a need for social change. Compares Awake to Hellman's The Little Foxes.

Schiff, Ellen. From Stereotype to Metaphor: The Jew in Contemporary Drama. Albany: State University of New York Press, 1982.

Argues that Awake and Sing! developed the prototypes of the dynamic Jewish mother, the bewildered father, the discontented daughter, and the sensitive and restless son. Believes that Awake's success is due largely to the Jewishness of its characters. Less enthusiastic praise for The Flowering Peach which uses "hackneyed Yiddish speech patterns" (41).

Young, Stark. "Awake and Whistle At Least." New Republic 82

(13 Mar. 1935): 134.

While praising Awake generally, comments upon two basic problems in the play: an overuse of guttural, common language, and superficial situations.

Not Examined

Robinson, LeRoy. "A Note on Language and Structure in Odets' Awake and Sing!" Kyushu American Literature 18 (1977): 40-44.

See also "An Exciting Dramatist Rises in the Theater." (Lefty).

See also Brown, John Mason. Broadway In Review. (Rocket).

See also Dozier, Richard J. "Recovering Odets' Paradise Lost." (Paradise).

See also Flexner, Eleanor. American Playwrights: 1918-1938. (Lefty).

The Big Knife (1949)

Atkinson, Brooks. "The Big Knife." New York Times 6 Mar. 1949, sec. 2: 1.

Discusses Odets' attack against Hollywood and how it misses its target. Finds parallels with Clash by Night -- both are not coherent works of art. Argues that Odets fails to make us sympathize with the play's protagonist; he is not likable enough. Praises characters and dialogue, but finds the play melodramatic

and lacking in the universal implications that Odets
thinks it has.

---. Rev. of The Big Knife. National Theatre, New York. New
York Times 25 Feb. 1949: 27.

Argues that Odets is more effective with individual
scenes than with the play as a whole. Faults Odets for
refusing to construct the play simply and for many
circumlocutions in dialogue. Notes that the play's
basic weakness is its characters; they are
"undistinguished and unattractive" and can scarcely
sustain the significance of the moral tragedy that Odets
tries to create. Likens the play to melodrama.

Barnes, Howard. "With A Dull Edge." Rev. of The Big Knife.
National Theatre, New York. New York Herald Tribune 25
Feb. 1949.

Regards the play as "dramatic hodge-podge," with poor
dialogue and an attack against Hollywood that misses its
mark.

Brown, John Mason. "Biting the Hand." Saturday Review of
Literature 32 (19 Mar. 1949): 34-35.

Views the play as a bitter, autobiographical,
overstatement of Odets' Hollywood years. Notes that
Odets erred in building the play around an actor instead
of a playwright. Review reprinted in: Still Seeing
Things. New York: McGraw Hill Co., 1950.

Chapman, John. "Odets Cuts Hollywood, Garfield His Veins in

Big Knife; No Blood." Rev. of The Big Knife. National
Theatre, New York. Daily News 25 Feb. 1949.

Notes a lack of sympathy for the main character.

Clurman, Harold. Lies Like Truth. New York: MacMillan,
1958. 49-57.

A compilation of theatre reviews previously published in
periodicals, such as Tomorrow Magazine, New Republic,
and The Nation. Notes structural weaknesses in Knife,
yet considers it an important play. Equates protagonist
with Odets; flaws in play are really flaws in Odets'
character. Comments that The Country Girl works because
of its uncomplicated characters. Notes allegory in
Peach, describing it as a play which represents a
"spiritural transition" in Odets (56).

---. "Sins of Clifford Odets." New Republic 14 Mar. 1949:
28-29.

Notes lack of coordination between plot and theme in
Knife.

Coleman, Robert. "Odets' The Big Knife Is Dull and
Confused." Rev. of The Big Knife. National Theatre,
New York. Daily Mirror 25 Feb. 1949.

Argues that the play is contrived, confusing, and dull.
Faults Odets for stilted dialogue.

Garland, Robert. "An Over-Produced and Overwritten Play."
Rev. of The Big Knife. National Theatre, New York. New
York Journal American 25 Feb. 1949.

Argues that the play is "showy [and] superficial" and does not create any sympathy for its main character.

Hawkins, William. "Big Knife Cuts Deep Into Human Folly." Rev. of The Big Knife. National Theatre, New York. New York World-Telegram 25 Feb. 1949.

Praises the play for its explosive ending, development of tension, and treatment of "the worship of Mammon" in Hollywood.

Morehouse, Ward. "Odets's Worst: The Big Knife." Rev. of The Big Knife. National Theatre, New York. The New York Sun 25 Feb. 1949.

Contends that the play is plotty, weighty, and overwritten. Expresses a disappointment in Odets' abilities at this point in his career.

Peck, Seymour. "An Angry Man From Hollywood." New York Times 20 Feb. 1949, sec. 2: 1+.

Odets defends The Big Knife, claiming it is not anti-Hollywood. Traces history of the play.

Watts, Richard Jr. "An Untriumphant War Against Hollywood." Rev. of The Big Knife. National Theatre, New York. New York Post 25 Feb. 1949.

Argues that the play is contrived, unbelievable, and melodramatic. Notes Odets' failure at attempting to use Hollywood as a symbol for a troubled America.

<u>Clash by Night</u> (1941)

Anderson, John. "<u>Clash by Night</u>." Rev. of <u>Clash by Night</u>.

> Belasco Theatre, New York. <u>New York Journal American</u> 29

> Dec. 1941.

> Argues that the play is evidence that Odets' talent has

> declined; his themes are virtually worthless.

Atkinson, Brooks. Rev. of <u>Clash by Night</u>. Belasco Theatre,

> New York. <u>New York Times</u> 29 Dec. 1941: 20.

> Argues that individual scenes are better than the play

> as a whole. Comments that the first half of the play is

> not only first-rate Odets, but some of the best writing

> done in modern drama. Praises Odets' characters and

> dialogue. Describes the story as engrossing, but the

> conclusion as obvious and the theme commonplace.

---. "Please Change the Scene." <u>New York Times</u> 11 Jan. 1942,

> sec. 9: 1.

> High praise for Odets' decision to use an unconventional

> setting and his genius for character development.

> Argues that the play's conclusion is merely there to end

> the play and that the play, ultimately, leaves one very

> unsatisfied.

Brown, John Mason. "Mr. Odets' <u>Clash by Night</u>." Rev. of

> <u>Clash by Night</u>. Belasco Theatre, New York. <u>New York</u>

> <u>World-Telegram</u>. 29 Dec. 1941.

> Contends that the play is slow-moving, pointless, and

completely lacking of the "Odets magic" that was present in almost all of his previous plays.

Kronenberger, Louis. "Odets, Where Is Thy Zing?" Rev. of Clash by Night. Belasco Theatre, New York. PM 29 Dec. 1941.

Finds the play to be dull, overwritten, and anti-climactic.

Lockbridge, Richard. "Clash by Night Opens at the Belasco." Rev. of Clash by Night. Belasco Theatre, New York. New York Sun 29 Dec. 1941.

Argues that the play offers little more than an uninteresting reworking of familiar material.

Mantle, Burns. "Domestic Tragedy Is Still Odets' Worry in His Clash by Night." Rev. of Clash by Night. Belasco Theatre, New York. New York Daily News 28 Dec. 1941.

Despite praise for Odets' dialogue and character development, finds the play uninteresting and "completely unrelieved in mood and tone."

O'Hara, John. "Desire Under the Rose." Newsweek 12 (Jan. 1942): 46.

Suggests that Odets reevaluate his playwriting abilities lest he present another play like this one. Cites cyclical speech and monotony of production.

Waldorf, Wilella. "Clash by Night." Rev. of Clash by Night. Belasco Theatre, New York. New York Post 29 Dec. 1941.

Finds the play tiresome and faults Odets for pretentious

dialogue, especially when compared with similar
situations in <u>Awake and Sing!</u>.

Watts, Richard Jr. "Staten Island." Rev. of <u>Clash by Night</u>.
Belasco Theatre, New York. <u>New York Herald Tribune</u> 29
Dec. 1941.

Argues that the play is unmoving and superficial.
Expresses disappointment with Odets' lack of compassion
and understanding for generally undesirable characters.

<u>See also</u> Atkinson, Brooks. "<u>The Big Knife</u>." (<u>The Big
Knife</u>).

<u>See also</u> Odets, Clifford. "Genesis of a Play." ("Articles
By Odets").

<u>The Country Girl</u> (1950)

Atkinson, Brooks. Rev. of <u>The Country Girl</u>. Lyceum Theatre,
New York. <u>New York Times</u> 11 Nov. 1950: 10.

Comments that the play is Odets' best in years, and
perhaps of his career. Argues that the story is
ordinary and the artistry of the play lies in its study
of human desperation. Praises Odets' dialogue and his
knowledge of people.

---. "<u>The Country Girl</u>." <u>New York Times</u> 19 Nov. 1950, sec.
2: 1.

Describes the play as a "potboiler" with little general
significance and a commonplace theme. Yet, argues that
this is Odets' best play in years, surpassed only by

<u>Awake</u>. High praise for characters and the relationships
between them.

Aulicino, Armand. "How <u>The Country Girl</u> Came About."

<u>Theatre Arts</u> May 1952: 54-57.

Various quotes from those directly involved with the
production of <u>The Country Girl</u> are offered: Odets,
Strasberg, Atkinson, Boris Aronson (set designer), etc.
The complete text of the play follows, pp. 58-86.

Barnes, Clive. "Theater: Odets Brought Up To Date." Rev. of

<u>Winter Journey</u>. Greenwich Mews Theater, New York. <u>New
York Times</u> 13 Mar. 1968: 39.

Argues that Odets should not be updated -- he is a man
of the 30's, and the passage of time has not been kind
to his work. Notes the operatic quality of the
dialogue, but considers the play to be "overdrawn and
underdeveloped," and faults Odets' use of a "battering
ram technique" to force his tale on the audience.
Provides some misleading information on the name change
from <u>The Country Girl</u> to <u>Winter Journey</u>.

Barnes, Howard. Rev. of <u>The Country Girl</u>. Lyceum Theatre,

New York. <u>New York Herald Tribune</u>. 11 Nov. 1950.

Praises the play but finds it "lacking in the
proportions to which it pretends." Argues that the role
of Georgie Elgin is a poorly defined character.

Brown, John Mason. "The Man Who Came Back." <u>Saturday Review</u>

9 Dec. 1950: 26-27.

Comments that because of The Country Girl, Odets is back as a viable force in the theatre. Reviews Odets' career up to this point.

Chapman, John. "Clifford Odets' The Country Girl An Absorbing, Well-Played Drama." Rev. of The Country Girl. Lyceum Theatre, New York. Daily News 11 Nov. 1950.

Praises the play for its "absorbingly human" characters. Questions the appropriateness of the title.

Clurman, Harold. "The First 15 Years." New Republic 11 Dec. 1950: 29-30.

Describes The Country Girl as "lightweight Odets" (29). However, believes the play to be successful because of its lack of social commentary. Defines the play as an introspective drama.

---. "Theatre." Nation 214 (3 Apr. 1972): 445-46.

Describes background of Country Girl, plot synopsis, character study. Notes that the play focuses on human frailties rather than economics and/or politics.

Coleman, Robert. "Country Girl Is Effective Only Part of the Time." Rev. of The Country Girl. Lyceum Theatre, New York. Daily Mirror 11 Nov. 1950.

Argues that the play is, at times, unbelievable and embarrassing. Praises Odets' dialogue, but comments that it is not as colloquial as it should be.

Darlington, W. A. "West End Wire." New York Times 13 Apr.

    1952, sec. 2: 3.

    Brief review of Winter Journey. Describes the play as

    "ordinary stage hooey" and faults the conclusion as

    false and unrealistic.

Gassner, John. Theatre At The Crossroads. New York: Holt,

    Rinehart and Winston, 1960.

    Describes The Country Girl as "a rather strained work"

    (180). While conceding Odets' considerable talent,

    believes that Odets failed to live up to his reputation;

    this play is not nearly as good as Lefty or Awake.

    Notes mellowing in Peach which flaws the work.

    Describes lack of focus and weak conclusion in Peach.

Hawkins, William. "The Country Girl a Problem in Suspense."

    Rev. of The Country Girl. Lyceum Theatre, New York.

    New York World-Telegram 11 Nov. 1950.

    Argues that the extreme tension of the first act is lost

    in the second act when the play becomes contrived.

"London Sees Odets Play." New York Times 4 Apr. 1952: 21.

    Brief review of Winter Journey which notes that the

    British reviewers were more impressed with the actors

    than with the play.

McClain, John. "An Engrossing Show; Last Scene Not Needed."

    Rev. of The Country Girl. Lyceum Theatre, New York.

    New York Journal American. 11 Nov. 1950.

    General praise for the play. Observes that the play's

final scene may not be needed, but fails to say why.

Norton, Elliot. "Clifford Odets Sans Message." <u>New York</u>
<u>Times</u> 5 Nov. 1950, sec. 2: 3.

Traces history of <u>The Country Girl</u>. Odets, who is to
direct this production, discusses omitting any "social
significance" from the play in order to write a purely
theatrical piece.

Tynan, Kenneth. <u>Curtains</u>. New York: Atheneum Press, 1961.
Reviews <u>Country Girl</u> in England where it was titled
<u>Winter Journey</u>. Condemns those who dismiss the lack of
social significance in the play. Describes Ibsen-like
qualities in the play.

Watts, Richard Jr. "The Welcome Return of Mr. Odets." Rev.
of <u>The Country Girl</u>. Lyceum Theatre, New York. <u>New</u>
<u>York Post</u> 12 Nov. 1950.

Argues that Odets is an effective writer when, as in
this play, he abandons social concerns. Praises him for
making an old plot "dramatically arresting" and for his
skill at developing character.

See also Clurman, Harold. <u>Lies Like Truth</u>. (<u>Big Knife</u>).

See also Semple, Lorenzo, Jr. "After 15 Years."
("Biographical Materials").

<u>The Flowering Peach</u> (1954)

Atkinson, Brooks. "Flowering Peach." <u>New York Times</u> 9 Jan.
1955, sec. 2: 1.

Compares Odets' style between the early plays and the later works. Notes comedy in the story of a famous biblical character who speaks a modern vernacular. Argues that the play is a microcosm for the experience of mankind.

---. "Theatre: Family Life In Noah's Ark." Rev. of The Flowering Peach. Belasco Theatre, New York. New York Times 29 Dec. 1954: 19.

Describes the play as "beautiful" and "his finest." Notes maturation in dialogue since the days of Awake. Finds the first half of the play more endearing; the second half is described as "repetitious and garrulous." Argues that the play is Odets' testament to the wisdom of mankind.

Becker, William. "Reflections On Three New Plays." Hudson Review 8 (Summer 1955): 263-268.

Expresses surprise at the commercial failure of Peach. Praises the play for being conventional, but faults Odets for directing the first production of his own play. Argues that this play represents an opportunity for Odets to reverse his usual practice of using domestic drama as a general symbol of man's fate. Discusses his Jewish background and how it was worked into the play.

Brown, John Mason. "On the Crest of Waves." Saturday Review 15 Jan. 1955: 30.

Notes the "good humor, sense of wonder, and gentle affirmation" of the play. Argues that both acts are admirable.

Chapman, John. "Legend of Noah Becomes a Family Squabble in The Flowering Peach." Rev. of The Flowering Peach. Belasco Theatre, New York. Daily News 29 Dec. 1954. Argues that the play does not inspire because Odets gets sidetracked by family bickering.

Coleman, Robert. "The Flowering Peach Is An Interesting Play." Rev. of The Flowering Peach. Belasco Theatre, New York. Daily Mirror 29 Dec. 1954. Finds some good qualities in the play and Odets' attempt to humanize Noah, but ultimately contends that it was wrong of him to take liberties with the Biblical tale. Argues that the play may offend the devout.

Hawkins, William. "The Ark Sails Again in Flowering Peach." Rev. of The Flowering Peach. Belasco Theatre, New York. New York World-Telegram 29 Dec. 1954. Argues that the play is "amusing, warm and original" except when it attempts to moralize.

Hymes, Barry. "Twenty Years On a Tightrope." Theatre Arts Apr. 1955: 68+. Notes Odets' mellowness in Peach which astonished some reviewers. Believes that the play will finally mature Odets as a playwright. Focuses on strong sense of family in the play.

Kerr, Walter F. "The Flowering Peach." Rev. of The
    Flowering Peach. Belasco Theatre, New York. New York
    Herald Tribune 29 Dec. 1954.
    Argues that the play's moral takes too long to be
    revealed and that its constant quarrelling serves no
    purpose.

McClain, John. "Hail Artistry of Skulnik. Biblical Story by
    Odets Produced With Distinction." Rev. of The Flowering
    Peach. Belasco Theatre, New York. New York Journal
    American 29 Dec. 1954.
    Praises play despite "serious doldrums here and there in
    the story." Argues against finding any allegorical
    themes in the play; its moral is meant to be very
    simple.

Mitgang, Herbert. "Odets Goes to Genesis." New York Times
    26 Dec. 1954, sec. 2: 1+.
    Describes Odets' autobiographical additions to the Noah
    tale. Notes mellowing attitude compared with early
    plays. Also provides a brief history of the play.

Watts, Richard Jr. "Noah, the Ark and Menasha Skulnik."
    Rev. of The Flowering Peach. Belasco Theatre, New York.
    New York Post 29 Dec. 1954.
    Praises the play's opening scenes and its conclusion,
    but finds fault with its middle sections. Argues that
    Odets' attempt to contemporize the theme fails.

Whitehead, Robert. "Odets' Tale For Today. . . And Our
    Time." Theatre Arts Oct. 1954: 24-25.

    Author is one of the producers of Peach. Describes
    Peach as a timely play with a clearly stated theme:
    "man's responsibility to himself and the world around
    him" (25). Notes certain American characteristics in
    Peach: "rebelliousness, virility and violence coupled
    with tenderness, sentiment and humor" (25).

See also Clurman, Harold. Lies Like Truth. (Big Knife).

See also Gassner, John. Theatre At The Crossroads. (Country
    Girl).

See also Schiff, Ellen. From Stereotype to Metaphor: The Jew
    in Contemporary Drama. (Awake).

Golden Boy (1937)

Atkinson, Brooks. "Clifford Odets." New York Times 21 Nov.
    1937, sec. 11: 1.

    Argues that Golden Boy restores Odets' talent to the
    stage. However, this talent is still said to be
    immature. Praises the development of themes in the play
    and notes that this is Odets' first play that is not
    rooted in the class struggle.

---. Rev. of Golden Boy. Belasco Theatre, New York. New
    York Times 5 Nov. 1937: 18.

    Praises the play, but finds fault with its lack of
    simplicity and sometimes pretentious dialogue.

Brown, Ivor. New York Times 23 Jan. 1938, sec. 11: 1.

Reviewer is the drama critic for the London Observer.
Describes the first act as "brilliant," the love story
"perfunctory," and the conclusion "trite." Praises
Odets' writing of family scenes.

Chouduri, A. D. "Golden Boy: Public Face of Illusion."
The Face of Illusion in American Drama. New Jersey:
Humanities Press, 1979. 59-73.

Characterizes Joe Bonaparte as the first protagonist in
Odets' plays to demonstrate the tragedy of an illusion-
ridden life. Discusses the conflict between Joe's
private world and his public world -- his success
creates loneliness and a destruction of values. Shows
Golden Boy to be an allegory for American society.

"Golden Boy In London." New York Times 22 June 1938: 27.

Notes the vigor of Odets' writing and praises the Group
Theatre performers. Discusses the difficulties in
acting Odets' very American play for an English
audience.

Morgan, Charles. Rev. of Golden Boy. St. James Theatre,
London. New York Times 10 July 1938, sec. 9: 1.

Praises the play as a good theatrical piece with lively
effects and a good sense of setting. Comments that the
play "has at root the mentality of the films." Notes
that Odets pays too much attention to his setting and
too little attention to his central theme. Questions

the effectiveness and meaning of the play's ending,
calling it a sentimentalized <u>Candida</u>. Discusses Odets'
use of American boxing lingo and how it fails to
translate to a British audience.

Nathan, George Jean. <u>The Theatre In The Fifties</u>. New York:
Alfred A. Knopf, 1953.

Critiques 1953 revival of <u>Golden Boy</u>. Describes it as a
typical Odets drama, showing limited talent.

<u>Not Examined</u>

Gibbs, Wolcott. "The Ring and the Bow." Rev. of <u>Golden Boy</u>.
<u>New Yorker</u> 22 Mar. 1952: 54. (Revival by ANTA Playhouse)

Kosok, Heinz. "Clifford Odets' <u>Golden Boy</u>." <u>Das</u>
<u>amerikanische Drama</u>. Ed. Paul Goetsch. Dusseldorf:
Bagel, 1974. 149-69.

<u>See also</u> Burke, Kenneth. <u>The Philosophy of Literary Form</u>.
(<u>Paradise</u>).

<u>See also</u> Clurman, Harold. "Three Introductions." (<u>Awake</u>).

<u>See also</u> Flexner, Eleanor. <u>American Playwrights: 1918-1938</u>.
(<u>Lefty</u>).

<u>See also</u> Gassner, John. <u>The Theatre In Our Times</u>. (<u>Awake</u>).

<u>See also</u> Himmelstein, Morgan Y. <u>Drama Was A Weapon</u>.
(<u>Lefty</u>).

<u>Night Music</u> (1940)

Atkinson, Brooks. Rev. of <u>Night Music</u>. Broadhurst Theatre,

Argues that Odets' writing lacks discipline and that he is now writing like William Saroyan. Notes some good scenes but considers the play erratic and foolish. Comments that Odets cannot decide if he is a playwright or a "boogie-woogie musician."

---. New York Times 3 Mar. 1940, sec. 10: 1.

Notes Odets' writing style and how it compares (unfavorably) with that of William Saroyan. Argues that both playwrights are "lost in a haze of romantic mysticism." Describes similar scenes in Night Music and Saroyan's The Time of Your Life. Comments that Odets offers no mature ideas or guidance in the conduct of life, and finds the play not able to be taken seriously. While praising Odets' talents in general, argues that his style has now become a mannerism which no longer expresses a central theme.

Clurman, Harold. "Around Night Music." New Republic 30 (Apr. 1951): 22.

Determines why this play is "doomed to fail." Notes homlessness theme in play.

Dusenbury, Winifred L. The Theme of Loneliness in Modern American Drama. Gainesville: University of Florida Press, 1960.

Discusses homelessness in the play. Notes less of an emphasis on outside forces: battle is within the

individual. Rebuffs notion that protagonist is
unnecessarily belligerent.

Lockridge, Richard. "Clifford Odets Chronicles Young Love In
Night Music at the Broadhurst." Rev. of Night Music.
Broadhurst Theatre, New York. New York Sun 23 Feb.
1940.
Describes the play as "minor Odets" because it has
little to say and serves no great purpose other than to
entertain. Argues that the play focuses on individuals
rather than theme.

Mantle, Burns. "Night Music. Two On An Island, According to
Odets." Rev. of Night Music. Broadhurst Theatre, New
York. New York Daily News 23 Feb. 1940.
Argues that Odets holds faithfully to his social
concerns in a play which otherwise resembles Elmer
Rice's Two On An Island. Hints that the play may have
been written for Elia Kazan (who portrayed the leading
man).

Ross, George. "Odets' Night Music A Tour of Manhattan."
Rev. of Night Music. Broadhurst Theatre, New York. New
York World-Telegram 23 Feb. 1940.
Notes parallel with Elmer Rice's Two On An Island.
Finds the play confusing, diffuse, and "goofy." Odets'
ear for dialogue is praised.

Waldorf, Wilella. "Odets's Night Music Opens at the

Broadhurst." Rev. of Night Music. Broadhurst Theatre,
New York. New York Post 23 Feb. 1940.

Argues that the play is entertaining only because of its
varied characters. Complains that the play is talky and
lacks direction and focus. High praise for dialogue.

Watts, Richard, Jr. "Odets On An Island." Rev. of Night
Music. Broadhurst Theatre, New York. New York Herald
Tribune 23 Feb. 1940.

Comments that the play is too wordy and that Odets'
writing now resembles both that of William Saroyan and
Elmer Rice (especially Rice's play Two On An Island).
Notes that Odets is better at observation than
philosophy.

Not Examined

Kerr, Walter. "Night Music." Commonweal 54 (27 Apr. 1951):
58-59. (Revival by ANTA)

See also Brown, John Mason. Broadway In Review. (Rocket).

See also Odets, Clifford. The Time Is Ripe. ("Journals and
Diaries").

Paradise Lost (1935).

Atkinson, Brooks. Rev. of Paradise Lost. Longacre Theatre,
New York. New York Times 10 Dec. 1935: 31.

Describes play as Odets' "Chekhov interlude" and notes a
comparison between Paradise and The Cherry Orchard.

Describes the play as an exercise in style. Comments that Odets is still an immature writer whose "ideas about human beings are undigested."

---. New York Times 29 Dec. 1935, sec. 9: 1.

Argues that while the play proves that Odets is "no false alarm" as a playwright, it is inferior to Awake and Sing!. Praises the theme of the play but finds it "an inferior imitation of Chekhov," and immature. Notes that Odets has a better understanding of Jewish family life in the Bronx than the American middle-class in general.

Burke, Kenneth. "By Ice, Fire, or Decay?" The Philosophy of Literary Form. 2nd ed. Baton Rouge: Louisiana University Press, 1957. 429-32.

Describes the play in terms of a ritual of decay and rebirth. Demonstrates the symbolism of Golden Boy (33).

Dozier, Richard J. "Recovering Odets' Paradise Lost." Essays in Literature 5 (Fall 1978): 209-21.

Suggests that with "judicious editing and imaginative staging, [Paradise Lost] could challenge Awake as the best of Odets' early work" (220). Compares Paradise and Awake. Notes Odets' unrelenting faith in Paradise.

Fagin, N. Bryllion. "In Search of an American Cherry Orchard." Texas Quarterly 1 (Summer-Autumn 1958): 132-41.

Considers Odets to be the only Northern playwright who

has attempted to Americanize Chekhov's The Cherry
Orchard in Paradise Lost. Notes that he fails because
he misinterprets Chekhov's intentions and because
Chekhov is not popular theatre and should not be
imitated by dramatists (like Odets) who are trained in
popular theatre.

Garland, Robert. "Odets -- Where Is Thy Sting." Current
Controversy 1 (Feb. 1936): 32+.

Notes that Odets' future as a rising young dramatist is
in jeopardy because of this play. Faults complaining,
unrealistic characters and a defeatist attitude which
permeates the play. Notes the Chekhovian quality of the
play but complains that Odets has "one foot in The
Cherry Orchard and the other on a soapbox" (39).

Gassner, John. Dramatic Soundings. Ed. Glenn Loney. New
York: Crown Publishers, Inc., 1968.

Reprinted comments from "Paradise Lost and the Theatre
of Frustration" (New Theatre, Jan. 1936). Views
Paradise as an advance in Odets' evolution as a
playwright. Describes dramatic structure of Lefty.
Labels Till the Day I Die "a masterpiece" (447).

Morgan, Charles. Rev. of Paradise Lost. London. New York
Times 8 Jan 1939, sec. 9: 1.

Argues that Odets is not translatable (notes American
accents used by some English actors) due to Odets' ear
for the rhythms of American speech. Describes the play

as confusing and ambiguous and notes a flawed philosophy
in it. Expresses a strong dislike for the title because
it is identical to Milton's famous work.

Not Examined

Farrell, James T. Partisan Review and Anvil 3 (Feb. 1936):
28-29.

See also "An Exciting Dramatist Rises in the Theatre."
(Lefty).

See also Clurman, Harold. "Three Introductions." (Awake).

See also Flexner, Eleanor. American Playwrights: 1918-1938.
(Lefty).

See also Himmelstein, Morgan Y. Drama Was A Weapon.
(Lefty).

See also Isaacs, Edith. "Clifford Odets." (Lefty).

Rocket to the Moon (1938)

Atkinson, Brooks. Rev. of Rocket to the Moon. Belasco
Theatre, New York. New York Times 25 Nov. 1938: 18.
Argues that the play is too long and too complicated to
deal effectively with its central theme -- love.
Praises the first act as some of Odets' best work and
argues that the play falters in its final two acts.
Notes that Odets' unparalleled gift for dialogue works
against him; he fails to arrive at conclusions and his
dialogue is often tangential.

---. New York Times 4 Dec. 1938, sec. 10: 5.

Praises Odets' genius and the tendency of reviewers to lose faith in him when his writing falters. Discusses the energy of the play and Odets' gift for portraying people on edge about something without knowing what. Argues that Odets interrupts important thematic speeches with comic interludes. Comments that Rocket fails to clarify the theme of love and must be considered a failure as a result.

Brenman-Gibson, Margaret. "The Creation of Plays: With a Specimen Analysis. Psychoanalysis, Creativity, and Literature. Ed. Alan Roland. New York: Columbia University Press, 1978. 178-230.

Chronicles research into Odets' life in connection with Clifford Odets: American Playwright (see also "Biographical Materials"). Applies principles of psychology to Rocket to the Moon, showing Odets' psychological development as an artist.

Brown, John Mason. Broadway In Review. New York: W. W. Norton and Co., 1940.

Discusses the theme of love and how Odets attempts to use it in new ways. Praises dialogue in Rocket. Defines Awake as a Chekhovian play. Expresses disappointment in Night Music due to Odets' lack of maturity as a playwright.

Gilder, Rosamond. "Song and Dance: Broadway in Review."

   Theatre Arts 23 (Jan. 1939): 12-13.

   Brief "review" which praises Odets' "mastery of speech"

   in this play.

See also Dusenbury, Winifred L. The Theme of Loneliness in

   Modern American Drama. (Night Music).

See also Isaacs, Edith. "Clifford Odets." (Lefty).

See also O'Hara, Frank H. Today In American Drama. (Awake).

The Russian People (1942)

Anderson, John. "Simonov War Play Reveals Heroic Red Stand

   Against German Invaders." Rev. of The Russian People.

   Guild Theatre, New York. New York Journal American 30

   Dec. 1942.

   Argues that the play is static, episodic, and

   untheatrical. However, describes Odets' writing as

   "skillful," and "adroitly colloquial."

Barnes, Howard. "Soviet War Drama." Rev. of The Russian

   People. Guild Theatre, New York. New York Herald-

   Tribune 30 Dec. 1942.

   While citing the production as "effective," argues that

   the play is "sprawling" and "uneven." Faults Odets'

   adaptation as lacking in clarity and fluency, and

   complains about his use of English colloquialisms.

Kronenberger, Louis. "A Great Story Remains Untold." Rev.

of The Russian People. Guild Theatre, New York. PM 30

Dec. 1942.

Describes the play as "a grievous disappointment,"

citing Simonov's script as the major flaw. As for

Odets' adaptation, it is labeled "faithful and

competent."

Lockridge, Richard. "The Russian People, Soviet War Drama,

Is Offered at the Guild Theater." Rev. of The Russian

People. Guild Theatre, New York. New York Sun 30 Dec.

1942.

Praises the play for being "alive and vivid," although

finds the first act to be slow. Odets' contribution is

mentioned in passing.

Mantle, Burns. "The Russian People: Dramatic Report From the

Soviet Front." Rev. of The Russian People. Guild

Theatre, New York. New York Daily News 30 Dec. 1942.

Argues that the play is a "factual, day-by-day report"

of Russia's war effort, but considers it an impressive

account. There is no mention of Odets' contribution.

Nichols, Lewis. Rev. of The Russian People. Guild Theatre,

New York. New York Times 30 Dec. 1942: 17.

Argues that the play as a whole is not as good as its

best parts (which are very good). Notes that Odets

fails to solidify relationships and creates an

atmosphere of confusion.

Rascoe, Burton. "The Russian People Opens at the Guild."
Rev. of The Russian People. Guild Theatre, New York.
New York World-Telegram 30 Dec. 1942.
Faults the production for being uninspired and the play
for being unconvincing, trivial, and "a libel on [the
Russian people]." Although no credit is given to Odets'
translation, there is mention of an interview with him
in the Information Bulletin of the Soviet Embassy, which
served as the press kit for reviewers.

Waldorf, Wilella. "The Theatre Guild Presents Simonov's The
Russian People." Rev. of The Russian People. Guild
Theatre, New York. New York Post 30 Dec. 1942.
Finds the play disappointing: "interesting but hardly
arresting." Odets' contribution is all but ignored.

"Washington Greets New Russian Drama." New York Times 16
Dec. 1942: 21.
Provides a very brief plot synopsis of this Odets
adaptation and notes that the Soviet Ambassador and his
wife attended the premiere.

The Silent Partner (1972)

Clurman, Harold. "Found: A 'Lost' Play By Odets." New York
Times 30 Apr. 1972, sec. 2: 1+.
Announces intention of the Actors' Studio to do a
workshop production of this play. Discusses play's
history: originally intended for the Group Theatre,

needed revision. Complains that the play contains "too
many Odetsisms" and a heavy atmosphere of doom.

See also Brenman-Gibson, Margaret. Clifford Odets: American
Playwright. 411-417. ("Biographical Materials").

Till the Day I Die (1935)

Atkinson, Brooks. Rev. of Till the Day I Die. Longacre
Theatre, New York. New York Times 27 Mar. 1935: 24.
Describes the play as being inferior to Lefty and Awake
because it has less-developed characters and an
uncertain point of view. Notes communistic trend in
Odets' writing, but praises his playwriting ability.

Miller, Jeanne-Marie A. "Odets, Miller and Communism."
College Language Association Journal 19 (1976): 484-493.
Argues that Odets used his play Till the Day I Die to
warn audiences against fascism, which he viewed as being
as dangerous to America as it was to Germany. Discusses
the critical response to Till the Day I Die, one of the
first serious anti-Nazi plays.

See also Gassner, John. Dramtic Soundings. (Paradise).

See also Isaacs, Edith. "Clifford Odets." (Lefty).

See also Isaacs, Edith. "Going Left With Fortune." (Lefty).

See also Krutch, Joseph Wood. "Mr. Odets Speaks His Mind."
(Lefty).

See also Young, Stark. "Lefty and Nazi." (Lefty).

Waiting for Lefty (1935)

"An Exciting Dramatist Rises in the Theater." Literary
     Digest 6 Apr. 1935: 18.

     Outlines Lefty while describing Odets' seemingly
     overnight success.

Atkinson, Brooks. Rev. of Waiting for Lefty. Civic
     Repertory Theatre, New York. New York Times 11 Feb.
     1935: 14.

     Praises Lefty and Odets' talent as a writer. Cites
     revolutionary drama as a recent development in theatre.
     Also reviews sketches presented by the Group Theatre.
     Calls Lefty the "dynamics of the program."

---. Rev. of Waiting for Lefty. Longacre Theatre, New York.
     New York Times 27 Mar. 1935: 24.

     Offers a new appraisal of Lefty, calling it "one of the
     most dynamic dramas of the year in any department of our
     theatre." Notes that Odets performs as an actor in the
     "Interne Episode."

Dozier, Richard J. "Odets and Little Lefty." American
     Literature 48 (Jan. 1977): 597-98.

     Comments upon Gerald Weales' view that Lefty was based
     on Joseph North's Taxi Strike. Claims that Weales fails
     to explore this influence fully. Notes that cartoon art
     in propaganda publications may have inspired Odets'
     title.

Flexner, Eleanor. American Playwrights: 1918-1938. 1938.

New York: Books For Libraries Press, 1969.

Extremely high praise for and excessive quotations from
Lefty. Notes Chekhov influence. Less generous praise
for Awake and Paradise. Golden Boy, despite unclear
symbolism, seen as similar in intensity to Lefty.

Greenfield, Thomas Allen. Work and the Work Ethic in
American Drama, 1920-1970. Missouri: University of
Missouri Press, 1982.

Cites Lefty's influences as Rice's We The People and
Hauptmann's The Weavers. Labels Lefty the "most
important of the agit-props" (68), and the best in a
long line of plays which explored the significance of
the American worker in society.

Himmelstein, Morgan Y. Drama Was A Weapon. New Jersey:
Rutgers University Press, 1963.

Details the theatrical devices used in Lefty and how
Odets transformed the cartoon-like characters of agit-
prop into real human beings. Argues that Paradise has
no Communist raisonneur. Notes lessening of social
commentary in Golden Boy.

Isaacs, Edith. "Going Left With Fortune." Theatre Arts 19
(1935): 322-332.

Critiques of Lefty, Awake (very brief), and Till the Day
I Die. Comments that Lefty has "no clear outline or
point of view" (327) and has "no real worth as drama"
(328). Praises Odets' writing in Till the Day I Die,

rating it "far ahead of anything else that [he] has done" (328).

Kline, Herbert. "The New Plays." New Theatre 2 (Mar. 1935): 22-23.

Talks of Lefty and Odets' ability to achieve and maintain "absolute audience identification" (22). Notes flashback motif used in the play. Credits Odets as an important contributor to American revolutionary theatre.

Krutch, Joseph Wood. "Mr. Odets Speaks His Mind." Nation 140 (Apr. 10, 1935): 427-28.

Praises Lefty, and describes its structure as the "dramatic equivalent of soap-box oratory."

Lockridge, Richard. "Plays Of Protest." Saturday Review of Literature 19 (11 Mar. 1939): 13.

Review of The Best Short Plays of the Social Theatre (William Kozlenko, ed. New York: Random House, 1939) which includes Waiting for Lefty. Calls Lefty the best of those included "by a considerable margin" despite uneven scenes and an ending which utilizes "trickery."

Perelman, S. J. Waiting For Santy: A Christmas Playlet (With a bow to Mr. Clifford Odets). Twentieth Century Parody: American and British. Ed. Burling Lowrey. New York: Harcourt, Brace and Co., 1960. 189-192.

Parody of Lefty with Jewish gnomes working for Santa Claus complaining about their economic problems. Santa, also a Jew, is a villainous capitalist.

Pottle, Frederick A. "Drama Of Action." Yale Review 25

   (1936): 429-430.

   Book review of Three Plays (Random House) which focuses

   on Lefty. Predicts that Lefty is too dated to survive.

Seward, Lori and David Barbour. "Waiting for Lefty." Drama

   Review 28 (Winter 1984): 38-48.

   Discusses the history of the play, offers a plot

   synopsis, and reviews its impact in the United States

   and Europe. Also provides cast lists and pictures of

   both the original and Broadway casts.

Shuman, R[obert] Baird. "Waiting for Lefty; A Problem of

   Structure." Revue des Langues Vivantes 28 (Nov.-Dec.

   1962): 521-526.

   Argues that Lefty preserves its freshness and relevance

   despite the fact that the basic social issues of the

   depression era have faded. Disputes the critical notion

   that the play has structural problems. Concludes that

   if viewed episode by episode, the play is structurally

   sound.

Young, Stark. "Lefty and Nazi." New Republic 82 (10 Apr.

   1935): 247.

   Focuses on Lefty while dismissing Till the Day I Die.

   Notes that Odets does not exploit any movement or cause

   in Lefty, despite Marxist influence.

Not Examined

Grabes, Herbet. "Uber die Wirkungstrategie des Agitatorischen
     Dramas: Clifford Odets' Waiting for Lefty." Die Neuren
     Sprachen 24 (1975): 70-79.

Vietta, Susanne. "Formen der Sozialkritik in Elmer Rice's
     The Adding Machine und Clifford Odets' Waiting for
     Lefty." Geschichte und Gesellschaft in der
     amerikanischen Literatur. Ed. Karl Schubert and Ursula
     Muller-Richter. Heidelber: Quelle & Meyer, 1975. 188-
     210.

See also Atkinson, Brooks. New York Times 10 Mar. 1935.
     (Awake).

See also Clurman, Harold. The Fervent Years. ("Critical
     Studies: Politics and the Group Theatre").

See also Drew, Elizabeth. Discovering Drama. (Awake).

See also Gassner, John. Dramatic Soundings. (Paradise Lost).

Critical Studies: Politics and the Group Theatre

A listing of sources dealing exclusively with Odets' social outlook, the politics of the 1930's, or the Group Theatre.

Chinoy, Helen Kritch, ed. "Reunion: A Self-Portrait of the Group Theatre." Educational Theatre Journal 28 (Dec. 1976).

Entire issue devoted to the Group Theatre. Contains history, pictures, interviews, and biographies, not only of Odets but of Clurman, Strasberg, Crawford, Kazan, Gorelik, etc. Section on Odets hints that he could write only for the Group; without them, he was lost (495-500).

Clurman, Harold. The Fervent Years. 1945. New York: Da Capo Press, Inc., 1983.

Basic text on the Group Theatre. Provides personal insights on Odets: early years of playwriting, biographical information, character quirks, etc. All

112

plays produced by the Group are discussed as well as the
critical response to them. Dismisses Chekhovian
influence. Describes Odets' work as lower middle class,
not proletarian.

Cowley, Malcolm. "While They Waited For Lefty." Saturday
   Review 6 June 1964: 16+.
   Retrospect on proletarian writing and its place in
   American literature. Labels Odets a leader among
   proletarian writers. Disputes Clurman's claim that
   Lefty was the birth cry of a new era since it was not
   followed by similar works. Notes mood change in country
   soon after Lefty; social issues replaced by anti-Nazi
   sentiments.

Gagey, Edmond M. Revolution In American Drama. New York:
   Columbia University Press, 1947.
   Describes Odets as the most capable dramatist of the
   left. Comments that Odets was never a "complete or
   consistent Marxian" (173). Notes that Odets' later
   plays were leftist in sentiment only--a mellowing since
   Lefty and Awake.

Gassner, John. "Playwrights of the Period." Theatre Arts
   Sept. 1960: 19+.
   Argues that Odets abandoned realistic play structure in
   order to dramatize social realism. Describes Odets as
   the characteristic American playwright of the 1930's.

Notes, however, that social commentary could not sustain
Odets, leading to his downfall.

Goldstein, Malcolm. "Clifford Odets and the Found
Generation." American Drama and Its Critics. Ed. Alan
S. Downer. Chicago: University of Chicago Press, 1965.
Notes that Odets, in the late 1940's, was still writing
the plays of the '30's. Argues that he relied too
heavily on economic problems to sustain the plays.
Talks of Chekhovian influence. Comments that because he
failed to change the world through his work, Odets faded
out.

---. The Political Stage: American Drama and Theater of the
Great Depression. New York: Oxford University Press,
1974.
Complains about Odets' endings in almost every play.
Provides much information on the Group Theatre and the
critical response to Odets' plays. A good source for
individual play study.

Gorelik, Mordecai. "Legacy of the New Deal Drama." Drama
Survey 4 (Spring 1965): 38-43.
Notes a mellowing of Odets' political and social fervor
after Lefty and Awake. Reviews Gerald Rabkin's Drama
and Commitment. Discusses recent interest in the drama
of the 1930's.

---. New Theatres For Old. New York: Samuel French, 1940.
Argues that Odets shaped his plays on the resources of

the Group Theatre (actors, directors, designers, etc.).
Discusses allegory, psychology, and social significance
in the plays.

Gurko, Leo. The Angry Decade. New York: Dodd, Mead and Co.,
1947. 180-181.

Labels Odets "the official stage historian of the
proletariat" (180) and argues that his plays were
products of the depression and the New Deal. His films
are described as "interesting failures" (181). Text
contains errors in the chronology of Odets' plays as
performed.

Kempton, Murray. Part of Our Time. New York: Simon and
Schuster, 1955. 184-210.

Discusses the Group Theatre and its band of angry young
men who were loyal to both their cause and the theatre.
Notes that Odets sustained the Group through his very
successful plays (Lefty and Awake, primarily) and
describes the decline of the Group as a result of its
commercial success. Some information on Odets'
testimony before the HUAC, including quotes by Odets.

Kirby, Michael, ed. "The Group Theatre." Drama Review 28
(Winter 1984).

Entire issue devoted to the Group Theatre. Contains two
pieces specifically about Odets (see also Odets below,
and Seward, Lori [Lefty]). Also includes detailed

discussions of the Group and specific evaluations of
some of its most famous productions.

Lal, Malashri. "The American Protest Theatre." Humanities
Review 2 (1980): 16-21.
Argues that Odets demonstrated that "protest" plays
could have an aesthetic value. Focuses on the literary
value of, primarily, Lefty and Awake, while commenting
that Odets' political ideology never took roots in
America. Some biographical information.

Levine, Ira A. Left-Wing Dramatic Theory in the American
Theatre. Michigan: Umi Research Press, 1985.
Argues that Odets' plays had an important influence on
the artistic direction of radical drama. Describes his
style in Lefty as a blend of agit-prop and realism.
Discusses the rise of the Group Theatre, its successes,
and its "mutually supportive relationship" with Odets
(83).

Mendelsohn, Michael J. "The Social Critics On Stage."
Modern Drama 6 (1963): 277-85.
Argues that despite his later works, Odets will only be
remembered as a writer of the 1930's. Notes that Odets,
while attracted to proletarianism, was really a middle-
class writer. Discusses Chekhovian influence.

Odets, Clifford. "From the Group's Daybook." Drama Review
28 (Winter 1984): 3-5.
Excerpts of Odets' comments in the 1931 Daybook of the

Group Theatre, an ensemble journal which contained entries by all of its members. Odets, a 25-year old actor at the time, offers his personal views on the Group and its significance to him.

Rabkin, Gerald. <u>Drama and Commitment</u>. Bloomington: Indiana University Press, 1964.

Describes Odets' work as Marxist, not strictly proletarian. Argues that Odets' impact as a dramatist was lost as his commitment to social causes dwindled. Discusses allegory, social metaphors, and Hollywood "sell-out."

Smiley, Sam. <u>The Drama of Attack</u>. Columbia: University of Missouri Press, 1972.

Notes proletarian subject matter in Odets' early plays. Argues that Odets knew that capitalism was inevitable, but wanted to readjust it to better suit the middle-class.

Weales, Gerald. "The Group Theatre and Its Plays." <u>American Theatre</u>. Eds. John Russell and Bernard Harris. New York: St. Martin's Press, 1967.

Provides history and purpose of Group Theatre and lists all of its productions. Considers Odets the best playwright of the Group Theatre. Discusses how every Group Theatre play was a reflection of the organization itself. Concludes that both the plays and the Group were "successful failures" (85).

See also Miller, Arthur. <u>Timebends: A Life</u>. ("Biographical
Materials").

House Un-American Activities Committee

A brief listing for those interested in information or excerpts from Odets' 1952 testimony before the HUAC.

Bentley, Eric, ed. Thirty Years of Treason. New York: The Viking Press, 1971.

Excerpts from Odets' testimony (498-533) make this the best reference short of the transcripts themselves. Excerpts provide valuable biographical material and character insights. Bentley notes Odets' tendency to embellish or change details; suggests Gerald Weales' Clifford Odets: Playwright ("Critical Studies: General. 1964-Present") for clarification.

Goodman, Walter. The Committee. New York: Farrar, Straus and Giroux, 1968.

Odets is named a Communist by Ginger Rogers, Jack L. Warner, and Elia Kazan. Notes that Odets was the best-known and most successful "Communist writer" to testify.

"Odets and the Comrades." Newsweek 2 June 1952: 23.

119

Odets' testimony is shown to be a complete turnaround
from his philosophies of recent months: Odets wrote
articles for a leftist newspaper (The Daily Compass),
praising known Communist J. Edward Bromberg. Also,
Odets issued a statement defending 11 Communist members
on trial for conspiracy in 1950.

Not Examined

United States. House of Representatives. House Committee on
    Un-American Activities. "Communist Infiltration of the
    Hollywood Motion-Picture Industry." Hearings. May 19-
    21, 1952: 3453-3512.

United States. House of Representatives. House Committee on
    Un-American Activities. "Communist Infiltration of the
    Hollywood Motion-Picture Industry." Hearings. Jan. 28,
    1952: 2316.

See also Appel, Benjamin. "Odets University."
    ("Biographical Materials")

See also Clurman, Harold. All People Are Famous.
    ("Biographical Materials")

See also Kempton, Murray. Part of Our Time. ("Politics and
    the Group Theatre").

Dissertations

A listing of doctoral dissertations dealing exclusively with Clifford Odets.

Cantor, Harold. "Clifford Odets: Playwright-Poet." <u>DAI</u> 36 (1975): 1499A. SUNY, Binghamton.

    Eventually worked into 1978 book (<u>see also</u> "Critical Studies: General").

Chen, William Ching-Chi. "Clifford Odets and Ts'ao Yu: American and Chinese Dramatists of Social Protest." <u>DAI</u> 42 (1981): 268A. University of Minnesota.

    Compares Odets to Chinese playwright Ts'ao Yu, who, like Odets, was a social protest writer. Discusses their use of the Marxist doctrine and the solutions that each have found to remedy the ills of their respective social systems.

Dozier, Richard J. "The Early Plays of Clifford Odets." <u>DAI</u> 35 (1974): 399A. University of North Carolina at Chapel Hill.

Evaluates Odets' early plays in order to illuminate his
artistry and downplay his politics. Notes major
discrepancy between early and later plays in terms of
criticism.

Kuryk, David. "Love's Thin Awkward Plant: A Study of the
Work of Clifford Odets In Regard to the Individual and
His Relationship to Society." DA 25 (1964): 2513A.
University of Wisconsin.

Attempts to correct the viewpoint that Odets never
fulfilled his potential. Defends his reputation as an
influential literary figure.

Mendelsohn, Michael J. "Clifford Odets: A Critical Study."
DA 23 (1962): 2137A. University of Colorado.

Attempts to remove Odets from the framework of 1930's
social protest writers. Notes Chekhovian influence and
Odets' influence on recent playwrights. Interview of
Nov. 10, 1961 appended to dissertation. (See also
"Odets At Center Stage." "Biographical Materials")

Sabinson, Eric Mitchell. "Script and Transcript: The
Writings of Clifford Odets, Lillian Hellman, and Arthur
Miller in Relation to Their Testimony Before the U. S.
House Committee on Un-American Activities." DAI 47
(1986): 2161A.

Argues that the HUAC functioned as a literary critic and
playwright that affected Odets' writing considerably.
The Big Knife and The Country Girl are analyzed as pre-

testimony evidence, and The Flowering Peach as an after-
testimony example. Notes Odets' tendency to transform
testimony into allegory.

Sheldon, Neil. "Social Commentary In The Plays of Clifford
Odets and Arthur Miller." DA 24 (1964): 3018A. New
York University.

Determines the social problems of Odets' and Miller's
eras; identifies these problems in their plays. Notes
his decline in terms of social commentary into the
1940's.

Shuman, Robert Baird. "Social Concepts in the Stage Plays of
Clifford Odets." DA 21 (1961): 3771A. University of
Pennsylvania.

States the overall social context of Odets' plays.
Presents Odets in relation to his times and evaluates
his plays as literature. Notes that Odets suffered from
comparisons of early work to later plays.

Tondras, Arthur. "The Liberal Paradox: Clifford Odets, Elia
Kazan, and Arthur Miller." DAI 41 (1980): 256A.
Indiana University.

Analyzes liberal politics in representative works by
Clifford Odets. Argues that historical movements and
visions of history in art are determined by human
desire. In Odets' work: desire for a truly homogeneous
culture.

Wagner, Arthur. "Technique in the Revolutionary Plays of

Clifford Odets." <u>DA</u> 23 (1963): 4023A. Stanford
University.
Notes Odets' influence on certain British playwrights.
Uses John H. Lawson's theories of playwriting as a guide
for studying the structure of Odets' plays. Notes
Chekhovian influence.

Wright, Donald Gene. "A Critical Examination of the Works of
Clifford Odets According to a Psychoanalytic Criterion."
<u>DAI</u> 31 (1970): 2952A. University of Southern
California.
Explores conscious and unconscious responses to Odets'
plays. Determines the most successful plays by this
criterion. Also evaluates the merits of critical
commentary. Most objective and scholarly critics:
Krutch and Gassner. Most successful plays: <u>Golden Boy</u>,
<u>The Big Knife</u>, and <u>The Country Girl</u>.

List of Periodicals Cited

American Literature [Durham,
 North Carolina]

American Magazine
 [Springfield, Ohio]

American Quarterly
 [Philadelphia]

California English Journal

College Language Association
 Journal [Baltimore]

Commentary [New York]

Commonweal [New York]

The Critic [Chicago]

Criticism [Detroit]

Current Controversy

Daily Mirror [New York]

Daily News [New York]

Das amerikanische Drama

Die Neuren Sprachen

Drama Critique [Detroit]

Drama Review [Cambridge]

Drama Survey [Minneapolis]

Educational Theatre Journal
 [Washington]

Encore [Raleigh, North
 Carolina]

Essays in Literature
 [Macomb, Illinois]

The Explicator [Washington]

Harper's [New York]

Hispania [Mississippi]

Hudson Review [New York]

Humanities Review [New
 Delhi, India]

Jewish Currents [New York]

Kyushu American Literature
 [Japan]

Literary Digest [New York]

Literary Review [Madison, New
    Jersey]

Los Angeles Times

The Markham Review [New York]

Modern Drama [Toronto,
    Canada]

Nation [New York]

New Republic [New York]

New Theatre [New York]

New York Daily News

New Yorker

New York Herald Tribune

New York Journal American

New York Post

The New York Sun

The New York Times

New York World-Telegram

Newsweek [Los Angeles]

Partisan Review and Anvil
    [New York]

Poet Lore [Bethesada,
    Maryland]

PM [New York]

Revue des Langues Vivantes
    [France]

Research Studies of
    Washington State
    University [Pullman]

San Francisco Examiner

Saturday Review [New York]

Saturday Review of
    Literature [New York]

Show [New York]

Sight and Sound [London]

South Atlantic Quarterly
    [Durham, North Carolina]

Stage [Greenwich,
    Connecticut]

Studi Americani [Rome]

Texas Quarterly [Austin]

Theatre Arts [New York]

Theatre Arts Monthly [New
    York]

Time [Chicago]

Times Higher Education
    Supplement [London]

Wilson Bulletin

World Film News

Yale Review [New Haven,
    Connecticut]

Index

Found Generation", 24,
114.

"Clifford Odets and the
Jewish Context", 21, 68-
69.

"Clifford Odets and Ts'ao Yu:
American and Chinese
Dramatists of Social
Protest", 121.

"Clifford Odets Capitalizes
His Whole Life", 41.

"Clifford Odets Chronicles
Young Love In Night
Music at the
Broadhurst", 97.

"Clifford Odets: First
Chapters", 54-55.

"Clifford Odets: From
Influence to Affluence",
51.

"Clifford Odets' Golden Boy",
95.

Clifford Odets: Humane
Dramatist, 17, 67.

Clifford Odets: Playwright,
17, 52, 66, 69-70, 119.

"Clifford Odets, Playwright,
Dies", 45.

Clifford Odets: Playwright-
Poet, 18, 63.

Clifford Odets: Playwright-
Poet (Dissertation), 121.

"Clifford Odets Sans
Message", 89.

"Clifford Odets: The
Artist's Commitment", 67.

"Clifford Odets' The Country
Girl An Absorbing, Well-
Played Drama", 87.

Clifford Odets: The Thirties
and After, 17, 68.

"Clifford Odets: The Tragic
Dilemma", 71.

"Clifford Odets tra New Deal
e Nazismo", 70-71.

Clurman, Harold, 15, 18, 20-
21, 22, 23, 34, 45-46, 60,
74, 81, 87, 89, 93, 95,
96, 101, 105-106, 111,
112-113.

Cohen, Sarah Blecher, 69.

Cohn, Ruby, 19, 20, 64, 74.